PERIL AT SEA

THE LIFE OF GEORGE GRAYDON

To Barbara
with kindest regards

Geo. L. Graydon

the Peppertree Press
Sarasota, Florida

The writer would like to express his sincere thanks and deep gratitude to the following people for their help in getting the myriad stories in this book together.

To my dear friend Louise Spellman for her many hours of editorial assistance, enthusiasm and patience.

To Mandy Sands, my Granddaughter who started this episode by researching my associates from the Rescue Ship Zamalek that may still be alive and well. I must admit that for fifty years I had deliberately wiped from my mind all the disturbing and often violent memories of wartime life at sea.

To my daughters Wendy Brecht and Carol Exell for their help in remembering some of their early memories.

To my good friend Mike McDermott for his recollections of earlier meetings and subsequent happy adventures together.

Without this help and encouragement, I would never have managed to correlate the articles in this book so well.

A LIFE AT SEA

March 2014

I first went to sea as a deck boy in 1936 on the *S.S. Woodcock*, owned by the General Steam Navigation Company of Leith, Scotland. The ship did a regular trip from Leith to London with general cargo including trucks. Life for my family as a whole was no worse than some, but my early recollections of our life, which started in the very early years of the Depression, was a kaleidoscope of misery, poor food, few clothes, and the drudgery of helping in the house, washing floors, cleaning windows, and looking after crying little kids. Mother suffered from a continuous stream of weird and wonderful ailments, plus birth control at that time was a mystery, vaguely heard about. My father had a major problem getting work of sufficient worth during this time, and nine of us subsisted on his wages of £2 sterling a week. To eke out the meagre income at home, I managed to get a job with a local bakery delivering breakfast rolls to customers' doors. This meant that I had to rise at 5:15 a.m. every morning in order to be at the bakery, load up, and start delivering rolls by 5:45 a.m. Delivery took about an hour and ten minutes. On bitter winter mornings it was sheer misery, as I had no heavy clothing and wore boots that were falling apart. I had to rush home, have tea and toast, and then rush to school. On reaching 14 years of age, my father got me a job in the electrical engineering firm of Bruce Peebles, who manufactured large electrical motors. I desperately wanted to work in the engine-building department, but was sent to a section bossed by a lady forewoman and a female assembly crew. I was given the job of straightening out copper strips 1 inch wide by 3/16 inches thick and 6 feet long. To accomplish this we had to raise the strips and smash them down on a heavy steel bench. The physical agony of doing this all day long, coupled with the monotony of the repetitive work of pounding the bench, was soul destroying. I requested a transfer to the engine-building shop numerous times and was turned down and told to get back to work. The forewoman seemed to be forever finding fault and telling us off. Life did not seem to be worthwhile! One day another apprentice and I decided to play a trick on the forewoman. We went to the furnaces where the shellac was used to bake around the copper armatures as an insulator. We picked up two handfuls of semi-liquid shellac and stuffed it in her work shoes. We waited for an explosion of wrath, but this lady being a large and dour Scotswoman said not a word and carried on all day as if nothing had happened, but come finishing time serious trouble erupted as the shellac had solidified and the shoes had to be cut off her feet. Next morning we were marched to the office where we were told we were to be handed to the police to be dealt with. We were then asked who was going to pay for new shoes, stockings, and the doctor's bill. My father was called and I was fired. How he dealt with the problem I never did find out, but the loss of income to the family was hammered home to me in no uncertain terms. I then got a job with a licensed greengrocer delivering shopping; as it did not pay very well I kept looking around until I obtained a better paying job as a bicycle repair mechanic and delivery boy. Finally, after a series of odd jobs, my father got me a job as a deck boy on the *S.S. Woodcock*.

When I joined the *S.S. Woodcock* as a deck-boy, I thought that I had found a way to escape from hell at home. Little did I know what a terrible time I was in for! I was paid one pound, nine shillings a week. My mother demanded that I pay her 12 shillings a week out of this meagre sum. Naturally, that did not leave much for me to live on. Then I had to buy, store, and cook my own food, buy clothes, heavy weather gear, towels, toiletries, and more. I lived on tea and jelly sandwiches for a while before some of my shipmates started to teach me how to operate cheaply. Plus, they quietly plied me with the odd bowl of soup that they said they did not want. Only much later did I realize their generosity in taking me under their wing, so to speak. The shock of going from an ordinary life ashore to one at sea for a very young boy was horrendous. The lack of sleep, due to a routine of four hours on and four hours off for twenty four hours of every day at sea, together with seasickness, cold, wet, hunger, and the atrocious weather in the North Sea, where winds from Siberia and the Baltic Ocean chilled air and water to a miserable degree. On coasting vessels nothing was provided by the ship owners for the deck crew or firemen. By the time you came off watch, usually wet, cold, miserable, and with soaking wet clothes, stripped off, made something to eat, then staggered into your bunk for about two hours sleep before being rousted out to dress and eat before your next watch, which consisted of a two-hour stint at the wheel of the ship with an hour on lookout, which was usually a little perch right up in the bow of the ship. Lord help you if the mate on watch on the bridge saw a light or anything unusual before you did. I remember the bosun to this day, as he was a fearsome-looking giant of a man who had been a fisherman out of Stornoway. He had taken an instant dislike to me for some reason, and he made sure I got all the filthiest jobs he could find; these included raising steel covers and crawling through filthy scummy bilge water to locate the strum boxes, which were located in the deep bowels of the ship. These steel boxes were perforated with holes and designed to stop debris from being picked up by the pumps, which pumped filthy bile water overboard. If a canvas hatch cover was torn loose from the wooden wedges, I would be rousted out of my bunk to help the carpenter do the required repairs, and since this always happened in a howling gale I was a bundle of wet misery. No sooner did I get warmed up than I was given the task of cleaning the green verdigris from the brass ship's bell and the many brass portholes around the deck houses. This was done with a mixture of pumice stone paste and oil that made my already torn hands permanently black, broken nails and skin raw with salt water blisters. Then he put me to cleaning all the paraffin oil lamps, trimming the wicks and cleaning the lamp glasses, all with old rags or torn newspaper. Next he would send me into the bowels of the ship to clean out all the accumulated debris, then I had to go on my watch. A favorite trick of the bosun was to have me put a new bulb in the mainmast headlight which was at least one hundred and fifty feet above sea level that, of course, always happened in bad weather. I was terrified out of my skull, as the ship would be pitching and plunging into a bad sea while the masthead was describing a crazy figure of eight in the sky. The last fifty feet of mast had no handholds, and it meant that I had to stand on the crosstrees and try to gauge the swing of the ship and then jump to catch the backstay and shin up to the headlamp, hold on with my legs tightly wrapped around the backstay and get one hand on the lamp bracket, unscrew the three brass wing nuts, reach in and unscrew the light bulb, throw it into the sea, reach inside my jacket and get the new bulb out, screw it into place, replace the wing nuts, and then slide down the backstay all the way to the deck. Naturally two weeks previously we had coated the backstays with tallow and lampblack. God help me if I had missed my grip when I jumped for the backstay and fallen to the deck or worse, into the ocean. My hands were raw meat when I finally hit the deck. I lay there with seas washing over me, wet, miserable, terrified and shaking with fear, not a surprising reaction. I could not believe that I had had the nerve or the stupidity to do what I did under these conditions. I swore that I would commit mayhem before I would ever do that again. The dockyard later reported a distorted lamp cover, which allowed rain and seawater to penetrate the lamp holder and blow the bulb.

Next, I was given the job of scraping the teak hand rails, then sand papering them to get them ready for varnishing. Each one had to have seven coats of varnish. Each coat had to be lightly sanded when hard enough before the next coat went on. The teak decks had to be washed and holystoned every week. This was accomplished by pushing a heavily lead-weighted coir brush backwards and forwards with the grain of the wood, using a mixture of water and ground pumice stone or fine sand. Many times when the ship took a lurch I would go staggering to the rail or the nearest hatch, hanging onto the damned holystone having been warned in no uncertain terms that if it went overboard the cost would be deducted from my pay. At this time in my life, I was a scrawny, miserable wretch, underweight, undernourished, half-starved, and poorly clad. The effort required to do the work demanded of me took all I had, but something drove me on — sheer cussedness, I guess. I just kept going and would not let the work or the conditions beat me. It took quite a while to build muscles and stamina, but I made it eventually.

Living in such close quarters as we seamen and firemen did aboard ship was a very grim experience, as the caliber of men who made their living at sea was a great mixture of ignorant and uneducated people from the area closely associated with the docks and ships and shipping. The life was hard, the pay poor, and entertainment was nonexistent. Reading and card playing plus some scrimshaw work and belt making were the order of the day. Discipline aboard ship was strictly adhered to and as work was very hard to come by, in those days nobody wanted to be fired and therefore had to put up with working conditions that are unbelievable today. The stench of closed quarters, wet clothes, and often unwashed bodies, the noise of clashing false teeth and heavy snoring, with the ship lurching from wave crest to hollow and then smashing into the next wave while shipping tons of seawater on deck. Needless to say, this flood usually found its way into the accommodations and ended up sloshing around on the floor of our living quarters. Bunks were tiered above one another, and often as the ship dived into a wave trough those of us in the upper bunks were flung on top of the poor souls in the lower bunk. Couple this with watches which were four hours on duty and four hours off, twenty-four hours a day and seven days a week while at sea. As there was always someone off watch trying to sleep and someone trying to eat or read in the same area. This area was almost invariably in the bows of the ship, where the maximum movement was accentuated and the noise level of the ship crashing into the seas was a constant source of irritation.

While life was kind of grim on this ship, it had quite a few lighter moments. A couple of seamen took me under their wings and taught me the required nautical terms for the various bits and pieces aboard ship. They also taught me to make knots in rope, splice rope and wire cables, sew canvas, and box the compass. Engines and how they worked had always intrigued me. One day, the Second Engineer found me watching the engines and from then on he answered all my questions and went to the trouble of making sketches of the parts I did not understand. In addition, he owned a twin cylinder "Matchless" motor-cycle, which he kept in a locked shed on the dock. On my undertaking to clean and polish it, he took me on a number of runs to places of historical interest in the Highlands of Scotland. I was most grateful to him for his kindness and missed him when he transferred to a larger ship. He had, in addition, taken a lot of trouble to try to improve my diction and vocabulary which was, at the time, atrocious.

After two years aboard ship, I obtained a transfer to another ship called the *Fauvette*, which was a twin-screw motor ship. She was very flat-bottomed and was a miserable ship to steer. She had a tendency to sheer off course with no warning, which made a two-hour stint at the wheel extremely debilitating due to the extreme concentration required. It did have the consolation of going abroad to ports on the European continent, namely France, Portugal, Holland, Hamburg and Bremerhaven in Germany. This opened up a whole new world to me, whose schooling had been minimal in the extreme. Around this time I developed my interest in engineering and in the stars. The Second Engineer was studying for his Chief's Certificate and, because I was always asking him how the engines worked, he took the time to teach me the basics of both steam and diesel engines, together with their auxiliary equipment. He showed me how to strip and clean the Bosch diesel injectors that supplied metered fuel to each cylinder.

The concept of a triple expansion steam engines operation took a while to absorb but when the light finally dawned, I was off. Then, because the *Fauvette* was diesel engine I was intrigued by the method of starting a multi-cylinder engine of that size and discovered that they used compressed air which was stored in very large, strongly constructed bottles or cylinders. I was advised by some of the older seamen to buy eau de cologne at Woolworth's in the High Street in London. We would then barter it for cigars, plug tobacco, and cigarillos in Holland. These we would then barter in Bremerhaven and Hamburg for pens and cigarette lighters that had pictures of nude women floating in a liquid. We had a great time flogging them to some barrow boy merchants in Petticoat Lane, the famous London open-air street market. This opened up a fascinating new world to me. The practice of some of these salesmen was an eye opener. I learned to watch and count my change twice before leaving the stalls. After watching very carefully, I saw them lay all the change out on a flat surface then quickly flick a two-shilling piece up the sleeve. Another trick was to take up the slack in a jacket at the back, and then tell the client it was a perfect fit. Selling watches was a favorite trick. Two or three of the same style watch would be shown to the customer, but one would have no works in it. Some terrific rows took place but the barrow boys all stuck together, and a customer who complained did not get anywhere.

Life started to get much more interesting as I became slowly fitter physically and financially. I managed to buy a second-hand bicycle and was able to tour a great deal of London, especially the City Centre and the Riverside. I came aboard ship one day to discover my nemesis — the bosun from the S.S. Woodcock — had joined our ship. Life was not the same from then on and for some time. One evening I had dressed with extra care as I had finally managed to talk a waitress from the local Lyon's coffee shop into going to the cinema with me. Having spent considerable time and effort in dressing, I felt pretty good. On climbing the stairs out of the accommodation, the bosun was at the top of the stairs. He lifted his hand and whacked my head, mussing my hair and causing me to lose my balance. I fell down the stairs, cut my lip and bruised my eye, plus, my new overcoat was torn. I took off the coat and the bosun came down the stairs and made some snide remark. I have no clear recollection to this day of what happened next. I felt rage and saw blood red. The next thing I knew, I was held by two policemen while still trying to whack the bosun with a chunk of wood. Was I scared! There was blood everywhere, along with broken wood from the bench I had picked up and broken on the bosun. The police took us both to night court. When the magistrate heard the case and I had stopped sniveling and answered him as best I could, he finally said, "My understanding is that this little fellow did this to this big hulking brute?" The constable said, "Yes sir, but I believe that there was provocation." Some of the seamen had backed up my side of the story unbeknown to me. The magistrate told me off, then dismissed the case and burst out laughing, as did the two policemen. I could not believe my luck in getting off so lightly. When we got back to the ship, the mess was incredible and the boys told me I had gone berserk and smashed a six-foot bench over the bosun and used the broken pieces to club him into a sobbing, bleeding mess, knowing that if I did not finish the job he would beat the hell out of me. From then on, I realized, I had a violent streak and that I had better watch it. I also bought and carried a knife and a metal marlin spike in a sheath, which I swore I would use on anyone who ill-used me in future. From then on I had no more trouble with that bosun. Talk about the worm turning!

In early 1939 when we were in Hamburg and Bremerhaven we noticed the increased brutal activity of the young brown shirt brigade, as they were called. We were not surprised when war was declared with Germany. We continued to trade back and forth between London, Holland, France, and Spain and experienced the odd enemy plane flying over the ship and occasionally dropping bombs on us, which always seemed to miss us by quite a bit, but shook us up none the less. The ship was finally fitted with a four-inch Hi Lo angle gun suitable for anti-aircraft and surface shooting, as necessary. Shell racks were welded to the deck for ready use, and a large locker was requisitioned for the rest of the arms and ammunition. Our crew were given a quick course in gunnery by a naval petty officer who taught us how to lead the gun sight far enough ahead of the plane so that hopefully the pilot would fly into the area of flack created by the exploding shell and be damaged enough to bring the plane down. Needless to say, it took quite a while to become proficient enough to have the confidence that we would succeed. The enemy plane that created most havoc with us at that time was the German Stuka dive bomber. Apart from carrying bombs, it was fitted with heavy machine guns and a horribly high decibel siren that cut through the nerves like a hot wire and chilled the blood while the pilot was in his bombing dive on the ship. We eventually got to the stage where we accepted it for what it was and learned to tolerate the noise.

As the Germans were starting to invade the Low Countries we were leaving Amsterdam by the canal for home one day when we were denied the return of the breech block for the four-inch Hi-Lo angle stern gun by the Quisling dock master. The Captain ordered us ashore with a machine gun to manually secure it at gunpoint. This was my first taste of what the war would be like. Holland being a neutral country, they had made us surrender the four-inch gun's breechblock on entering the canal at Wymudien on the way into Amsterdam.

By this time I had passed my exams for Able Bodied Seaman and with it came a raise in pay which, though small, was eagerly awaited.

I found out that my aunt and her husband owned a pub in the East End of London on Victoria Road in Bow. Whenever I had a weekend clear I was invited to the pub, and then on Saturday nights I would earn a little extra money going around and collecting empty glasses, those being in short supply and the pub doing a roaring trade, I was kept busy. My cousin and her girlfriend invited me to a number of parties and a very good friendship developed.

Unfortunately, this did not last very long. When I returned from the next voyage, the sad news that greeted me was that the whole street where my girlfriend lived had been demolished in a big bombing raid, and the whole family had been wiped out. When I went to look, the whole area was a shambles of brick, pebbles, broken glass, and over the whole area the stench of blood, cordite, and decomposing bodies. I was extremely upset. The whole town was of course suffering, but the docks were the main target of the bombers. The majority of Londoners eventually made a home in the Underground tube stations and lived there on and off as the severity of the bombing dictated until the end of the war. It was a sad sight to see whole families carrying on under such trying circumstances. Walking around during an air raid of that magnitude was both foolish and of course forbidden, but when we were caught out on the street away from any quick access to an air raid shelter, all we could do was run until a warden or a policeman directed us to the nearest shelter. The thousands of anti-aircraft shells exploding in the air above us created a maelstrom of spent shrapnel which we often had to run through to get to the shelter. We would run holding a jacket or anything else we could find over our heads in order to catch, we hoped, any bits of shrapnel heading for our heads. It was, to say the least, an extremely frightening experience and drove home to us the depth of misery and terror the people of London and all other large cities suffered throughout the whole course of the war. Around this time my uncle died, and my aunt decided that with the heavy bombing and damage it created she had better move to the country and decided to buy a property in Edinburgh, where my family lived. Joyce, my cousin, got a job in a baker's shop called Mason's. She became friendly with the owner's son, whom she introduced me to. He and I became very good friends, and as it turned out I met his niece, now my wife, Margaret Mason. More on this happy event later! Around this time we often had to tie up to a mooring buoy in the Thames to wait for another ship to finish unloading at St. Katherine's Dock, which was close to Tower Bridge. A London River boatman taught me how to handle a wherry, which is a 17-foot flat-bottomed skiff of a type favored on the river.

This was accomplished with a 14-foot ash oar fitted

to a cutout in the stern of the boat. The oar had to describe a figure of 8. I took quite a while to master it in the fast current and chop on the river, but I became very proficient eventually.

I did not realize how dangerous it could be until one day the ship dropped me off with the wherry. I had to row or skull, as it is called, to get to the mooring buoy, hold the rope lanyard in one hand, and then jump onto the buoy. The current was swift as tide, current, and wind were all blowing in the same direction. Tugs and barges going up and down the river created lots of waves and I ended up underwater, clinging on to the buoy for dear life with the wherry trying to tear my arm off. Then the Captain eased the ship close enough for a seaman to sling a light heaving line to me. Attached to this was a cable, which I had to pull in and shackle to the buoy. It was a frightening experience, and the Captain made an order to have a second man in the boat with me from then on.

The convoy system on the coast was in effect by this time and the bombing of the ships was starting to be a major problem. Stuka dive bombers were the worst, as they had a siren installed on the fuselage and as they entered their bombing run and dive the scream of the siren was nerve wracking, especially as all ships were firing whatever armaments they had. Bombs were dropping and the planes were machine-gunning the decks of the ships.

On the east coast around the "Wash" area at night especially if it was at all foggy, German "E" boats used to tie up to a buoy and wait for a convoy to approach before starting up engines and roaring down between the two columns of ships, shooting at everything they could and throwing hand grenades on to the ship's deck. Tracer bullets were an eerie sight, but ricocheting bullets were a major problem aboard ships together with the spent shrapnel from the bigger guns.

We had a nerve-wracking experience one dark night just after a very bad attack. We heard the roar of marine engines and saw this shape loom out of the darkness, crossing our bows at great speed. All guns that could bear, blazed away. All hell broke loose, flares shot up, and we learned to our dismay that we had shot up an R.A.F. motor launch that had gone out to pick up some downed airmen; fortunately no one was killed.

At this time both German planes and E boats were dropping magnetic mines in the coastal channels. The steel hulls of the ships, when passing over or even close to a magnet mine, triggered the switch and blew the hell out of the ship. After a heroic effort by a mine disposal expert, a magnetic mine located on a beach was stripped without mishap and an antidote in the form of "degaussing" was carried out on every ship. This required a heavy cable to be passed full length under the hull to demagnetize her steel structure. Then the magnetic compasses had all to be recalibrated.

The final straw for me was steering the ship up the London River, the Thames, while a major bombing raid was taking place. The whole town appeared to be on fire, and that night the very large Tate & Lyle sugar plant was hit and on fire. The place looked like Dante's Inferno, with the water reflecting the fierce flames, bombs going off, and Ack-Ack guns firing and airplane engines screaming. From my place at the wheel, inside the enclosed sandbagged bridge where the helm was located, it was terrifying, plus the pilot was continuously requesting course changes to clear other ships and both sunken and floating debris in the river. The terror created by the combination of the bombing and the claustrophobic effect of feeling trapped in the wheel house and being unable to do anything but steer the ship was mind-boggling and terrifying.

Early in 1940 I decided I would try for a berth on a foreign-going ship, as they had two major advantages. One, a cook was employed with assistants and we would be fed by the Company, plus we would do four hours on and eight hours off with alternate days on the dogwatch where we changed over watches, some going 4 p.m. to 6 p.m. and others doing 6 p.m. to 8 p.m. As long as a ship was at sea we worked seven days and nights a week. This theoretically gave us more time for reading, writing, mending and washing clothes, and in my case, studying my nautical books, which at that time I was starting to collect.

Prior to joining the next ship we applied for entry to the Naval Gunnery School in the port of Leith, where the C.P.O. was a crusty old guy but knew his business. He drilled us mercilessly on loading, aiming, and firing the 4" ack-ack guns they had fitted to the stern of all foreign-going merchant ships. The rear decks had to be specially strengthened to take both the weight and the shock of the guns' recoil. We were also taught to use a .38 revolver, the .303 Enfield rifle, and the Thompson submachine gun. In addition, we were also given very strict training in setting the fuses on the shells for the 4" ack-ack guns.

I joined the *S.S. Darlington Court* in May 1940. We sailed part of the way across the Atlantic in a convoy bound for Vancouver Island to load timber. The convoy dispersed and we sailed independently for the Panama Canal. The weather in the North Atlantic was atrocious, continuous gales with mountainous seas. Finally the Chief Engineer informed the Captain we had engine trouble. It appeared that due to the pounding the ship had taken as a light ship in ballast, we had had a bad hammering and one of the tall holding-down bolts for the cylinder head had fractured with damage to the engine bed plate. The decision was taken to limp at slow speed to the Azores for repairs.

Our arrival there was something else. As we entered harbor we observed a German cargo ship at anchor in the bay and could not resist the temptation to train our unloaded four-inch gun on her. We were gratified to see the German crew scurry for cover, but was the Captain ever mad at us! He said that we could have caused an international incident.

It should be noted that as Portugal was neutral, she was obliged to allow any ship to enter port for twenty-four hours to carry out repairs. We learned that the German cargo ship spent the rest of the war there with the crew interned and on parole.

The Chief Officer decided to have us paint the hull,

as we were due to be at anchor for a while. We rigged scaffolds under the curve of the bow with guy ropes to pull us close in and started to paint. We had no brushes and had to use a rag, which we dumped in a bucket of grey paint, squeezed out the excess, and rubbed the rest on the steel plates. The rust and rivets played war with our hands, but it was warm enough to be able to lower the scaffold now and again and take a dip in the bay. About this time the bum boats started to hang around the ship. We discovered we could quietly trade paint for the local vino. We got so drunk on the rough wine that we fell off the scaffold into the water; the Chief Officer was having apoplectic fits. It took a while to live that down.

The repairs had to be carried out manually, as the machine shop ashore was not equipped to handle this size of a job. However, they did a marvelous job of cobbling things together, and we left three weeks later for the Panama Canal and Vancouver Island. The trip from the Azores Islands to the Panama Canal was marred by continuous bad weather with gale after gale from the northeast. In addition, we were getting constant reports of ships being sunk by torpedoes. When we finally reached the Panama Canal Zone entrance and the weather improved, we were able to spruce up the accommodation and dry out our clothes. The trip through the Canal was an awe-inspiring experience for those of us who had never been through it before. As the Americans ran the Canal in those days we were boarded immediately on arrival by a detachment of American soldiers, some of whom were stationed in the engine room with guns at the ready and the balance on the ship's bridge. When we asked why, we were informed that all ships transiting the Canal were dealt with in the same manner in order to avoid an act of sabotage which could block the Canal, possibly by a rogue ship being blown up in the middle of the Canal. On entering the first set of locks we were boarded by a crew of Panamanians who told us we were not allowed to work the ship through the locks of the Canal. We were delighted, as it gave us an opportunity to look around and appreciate the ease with which the electric mules held a five-thousand ton deadweight ship immobile against the thousands of gallons of water surging into the locks from the sluice gates, while the ship was being floated higher by the rapidly rising water. When my stint at the wheel came up I was intrigued, but not for long. The pilot was a crusty old guy and kept calling for course corrections and making remarks about my steering ability, plus mosquitoes were swarming in clouds around my sweating naked shoulders. At the exit from the Canal we topped up with bunkers, stores, food, and water. We proceeded up the west coast of the USA in fine weather with lots of sunshine, which we all enjoyed thoroughly. I had the unique experience of being the helmsman going into Port Alberni on the West Coast of Vancouver Island with the famous "Tug Boat Annie" as the Pilot. She must have weighed 280 lbs. and had to climb a rope ladder to get aboard ship from the Pilot boat, all this in thick fog. We got underway with the Pilot holding a stopwatch and pulling the fog horn regularly, using the elapsed time of the return sound to navigate the ship up the channel, frequently cussing me for even one degree off course. We could not see a thing but she got us safely moored with the aid of two tugs, and we started loading immediately. It was fascinating to see the very particular way the cargo was loaded. With my usual penchant for asking questions I learned all about the Plimsoll line on the ship's hull and the difference in specific gravity of both fresh and salt water.

I also learned all about the term T.P.I. or tons per inch immersion, the upshot being that the ship could be loaded deeper in the water in a fresh water area and would rise to her permitted load marks in the open ocean salt water.

After partial loading we left to go around the island to Nanaimo and Cowichin Bay on Vancouver Island to complete loading. On leaving Port Alberni I was elected helmsman again and almost had a heart attack when I saw the narrow channel we had entered by. A sheer cliff was on one side and a shallow reef was on the other. My opinion of that Pilot went from rigid anger at her cussing me to complete admiration for the job she had done in conning the ship up the channel in thick fog.

We were given shore leave in Nanaimo and ended up in a logging camp. There we witnessed a most interesting exhibition of tree topping by so-called "monkey men." They wore spikes on their boots which enabled them to literally run up the tree, flipping a loop of rope around the tree to maintain their balance. We thought that this was incredible as they had to carry a saw which was attached to the heavy leather belt they habitually wore. We also saw how the cut logs were drag-linked to the wooden spillways which were part-filled with running water. The rush of water together with gravity kept the logs shooting down to the river at a great speed. To see these guys log rolling and clearing big log jams and finally chaining the logs into the shape of a raft ready for the tugs to take the raft downstream to the saw mill was a mind boggling and learning experience. We joined a crowd heading for the mess tent when the lunch gong went. The cook said, "Two bits and eat all you want." We thought that we were in seventh heaven. Steaks one inch thick, creamed potatoes, green vegetables, then apple pie and ice cream with big mugs of coffee. We were replete, having eaten until we were overloaded. Imagine our amazement on seeing the majority of the lumberjacks going back for seconds. No wonder these guys could eat so much. Crisp, fresh outdoor air coupled with sheer manual labor used up calories rapidly. The Canadian people on the island were very hospitable and made us welcome wherever we went. We also acquired a taste for barbequed steaks and barbequed fresh-caught Pacific salmon. Before leaving Nanaimo we topped up with stores, bunkers, fresh food, and water. This included loads of fresh fruits of all kinds. To us this was some kind of manna from heaven.

We came back down the West Coast of the United States with reasonable weather, entered the Panama Canal with its marvelous engineering feats of the three sets of locks with the massive electric mules to position and hold the ship steady against the inrush of millions of gallons of water to the locks. As the Americans owned the Canal in those days, they had armed guards in the engine room and on the bridge the whole time we transited the Canal, all work being done by Panamanian personnel. We thought that this was great as we had time to see the scenery as we passed.

We learned that the millions of tons of water used to fill the massive locks were all from the three lakes situated between the locks. Rainfall in the Panamanian area is so great that there is an adequate amount of water to supply the whole of the canal's needs without the need for pumps.

The water supply to the locks is controlled by large sluice gates located in the lock gates. These are raised and lowered hydraulically. We found out that the whole of the canal system including the lakes is 95 feet above sea level. This feat of engineering is one of the Wonders of the World. On leaving the Canal Zone we sailed through the Gulf of Mexico and enjoyed the warm weather and tranquil seas. As soon as we crossed the Gulf Stream heading north for our rendezvous with the Atlantic-bound convoy off Halifax we hit bad weather, a real northeaster with freezing rain, sleet, and snow.

We joined the convoy off Halifax, Nova Scotia. The weather deteriorated quickly and became the usual North Atlantic pounding. We noticed the ship steadily taking a list to starboard. On enquiring of the 2nd Officer what the problem was he laughed and said, "You have not sailed on a timber-carrying ship before." When I said that this was my first deep-sea trip, he explained that as timber was relatively light compared with a cargo of ore or similar, they could load it on deck to about 8 feet high without affecting the stability of the ship. This was then strapped down with heavy chains and bottle screws for tightening up the slack. Due to this storm being from the southwest and persisting for a couple of weeks, the timber on the weather side was soaking up waters, and the extra weight on that side was causing her to list to starboard.

I was most grateful to this officer, as he realized from my numerous questions that I wanted to learn as much as I could. He found me a couple of old books on navigation, ship handing, and the rules of the road. Thereafter, every night on the midnight to 4 a.m. watch, he would question me on a subject he told me to read, then he started to show me how to find the star constellations and the individual stars used for navigation, etc. He also loaned me an old chart and a set of navigation tables with which to work out latitude and longitude. He told me to buy a cheap sextant and practice with it. When we arrived at Immingham and we discharged cargo, the crew were paid off as the ship was going into dry dock for repairs to her hull and engines. I was most sorry to leave and told the Second Mate how very grateful I was for his help and advice. He parted, saying, "You should think about going to nautical college for your officer certificate." I was speechless and thanked him for the thought.

In those days, Officer's Country was another world, and deck hands were not welcome.

The Seaman's Shipping Pool at Leith arranged for a number of us to attend again a refresher course at the Naval Gunnery School, where we were again taught how to aim and fire our 4" H.A. guns. Also how to fuse the ammunition for the various estimated heights of the attacking aircraft and how to handle an Enfield .303 rifle and fire, strip, clean, and reload various types of machine guns. After passing our tests we were given certificates by the head of the Naval Gunnery School, who wished us luck and said, "I know you will all need it."

The Seaman's Shipping Pool at Leith then dispatched three of us to join a brand new ship called the *S.S. Benalbanach* in Glasgow. She was a grand sight to see, but a seaman's nightmare, as she had derricks specially built and rigged to take on the discharge of one-hundred ton heavy loads, namely railway engines. The size of the blocks and shackles were enormous and required the special services of a seaman rigger who could splice two-inch wire cable then frap them properly to avoid wire ends catching on anything or anybody. A large steel fid and a 14-pound maul were required to part the cable lay-up. A number of us learned how to do this after a great deal of lost skin and blood.

We loaded two thousand tons of bunker coal as ballast and left in convoy for the Panama Canal and Singapore. After a great deal of activity by the escorts, who chased off a number of submarine attacks, we then carried on alone through the Atlantic Ocean and made passage through the Panama Canal then across the Pacific alone again to Singapore. While wartime conditions prevailed the Captain was good enough to honor the tradition of seamen from time way back of inviting King Neptune aboard to baptize those neophytes who had not yet been dealt with when crossing the Equator. We were copiously coated with shaving cream, then dunked underwater in a very large canvas tub of sea water. We were also told that we were very lucky to get off lightly, as in peacetime the ceremony was more vigorously pursued. We were fortunate to make that passage without being accosted by submarine attacks. We anchored out in the bay at Singapore and off-loaded the bunker coal. We seamen handled the cargo winches and pulled the big buckets of coal up out of the hold and dumped them in lighters alongside. This was very slow, tedious, dirty work, carried out in very hot and humid conditions. We could not swim off the ship to cool off or clean up due to so many sharks being around, so we had to make do with fresh water, which was always in short supply due to a problem with the desalination plant. Our trips ashore were extremely interesting, especially to the local markets, which were colorful, noisy, dirty, and extremely odorous. The main drainage ditches lined the highways and byways, their purpose being to take away the flood water from the frequent tropical downpours. Trash and decomposing vermin choked most of them. This added to the odorous miasma that rose from the muddy ditch.

It took me three days of haggling with a local merchant to buy a set of matching cowhide suitcases. The crowd that gathered while the merchant and I traded words was highly amused. I called him every word short of thief that I could think of and he did likewise. It was great fun, as I ended up paying less than half what he had asked for at the start of our trading session.

We also discovered a merchant who would trade Siamese silver jewelry and opals for clothes in good condition. Needless to say, we left Singapore with very little left in the way of clothes and shoes.

We left Singapore for South Western Australia, where we loaded a few thousand tons of manganese ore. This acted as ballast as we headed for New Zealand to pick up a full cargo of wool.

While in Walaroo and Port Augustus we celebrated the New Year with the local Australians, who made us all extremely welcome. We partied every night at a different location. We found out how well these Australian miners could drink and hold their liquor. We tried to emulate them and suffered accordingly. Being seasick had nothing on the way we felt. I was sure I had no stomach lining left. In addition to liquor we were drinking the famous Australian wine called Plonk like it was water. Since it was high summer there at that time, we were very thirsty and the wine tasted heavenly, with drastic results.

En route from New South Wales we were diverted to the harbor at Hobart in Tasmania to use our paravanes to sweep for mines. We were informed that a Japanese submarine had dropped mines there.

On cutting a couple of mines loose we were ordered to shoot at them with our .303 Enfield rifles. Not only could I not hold the rifle steady, I also could not stop throwing up. Nothing would stay down in my tortured stomach, and my head was bursting. The Captain had to send an officer with a machine gun to explode the mines. He then gave us a lecture; I can still remember particularly the blistering language he used.

We then proceeded to Picton in the South Island to start loading wool as cargo. In Picton, which is located at the head of a deep sound in the north end of South Island, we met a group going to a big outdoor party and were invited to join them, which we did. Did we have fun! I met a young lady who was the daughter of the Manager of the New Zealand Shipping Company. He eventually offered me a job, which I had to regretfully decline. The young lady, it turned out, was visiting her grandparents who had a farm up-country. I was invited to visit them and stay the weekend. The Chief Officer gave me permission and off I went. We had a great time and I ended up falling off a horse so many times I still hate the damned things. It did create a source of hilarity among all and sundry. Sue promised to meet me in Wellington, but I thought it would never happen and felt quite devastated at leaving.

From there we sailed to Windy Wellington in the south end of the North Island for more cargo.

To my complete surprise, Sue was among the crowd waving from the dockside when we berthed. Again I received grudging permission to take time off from the Chief Officer. We took off for her home and met her parents and younger brother. We attended a number of parties and had a wonderful time. At this time I was running extremely short on cash. When going into a pub at lunch time for a beer and enjoying the free lunches served by the pub, I got into conversation with the barman and discovered that he was willing to pay good money for the Siamese silver jewelry we had. We were pleasantly shocked and amazed at the prices he quoted us. Fortunately I had enough sense to keep back enough to take home to the family as souvenirs.

The welcome we encountered everywhere we went was marvelous. From Wellington we finished loading at Christchurch in the South Island. We continued our partying in Christchurch as Sue had again managed to join us there. We were invited to lunch aboard one of her father's company's ships. We were astonished at the luxury of the type of accommodation provided for all hands, together with the quality and quantity of the food. It was like a fairy tale compared to wartime Britain and British ships.

We had received a warning of suspected German Q ship activity off the African coast and extremely strict instructions were issued to all and sundry that no trash of any kind was to be thrown overboard, as any flotsam like this would be a good indication to a German raider that a ship was in the vicinity, and no lights of any kind were allowed to be shown. If an engineer or a fireman dropped a wrench or a shovel on the decking a severe reprimand was inevitable, as sound carries a long way in and over water.

We then set off for Great Britain by way of the Cape of Good Hope. The trip across the Indian Ocean was sweltering, to say the least. We had a following breeze for most of the way that made for stagnant conditions aboard ship breeze-wise. Air conditioning was both non-existent and unheard of in British ships at that time. In addition, the glare from the ocean surface and clear blue sky created a nightmare condition for the eyes. Sunglasses were not only unheard of but were considered less than manly by the so-called macho men of the British Merchant Marine. I and a few other men ended up with a monumental headache that persisted until we hit cooler conditions above the equator. Tempers were short and everyone was snarling at one another due to the heat and stuffiness of the closed up-crew quarters. We sailed into the bay at Capetown and were fortunate to see Table Mountain without its so-called perpetual cap of cloud. After bunkering and taking on fresh provisions and topping up with water from the lighters we set off to make our passage to Halifax, Nova Scotia, to join the ocean convoy with escorts for the trip across the Atlantic to Great Britain and home. On route to Halifax, Nova Scotia, we ran into a storm of hurricane proportions just south of the Grand Banks off Newfoundland. The seas were mountainous and the wind was bitterly cold. A sea, which was estimated at nearly sixty feet in height, swept up on us from astern and we dropped into the deep trough of the wave with a sickening lurch, then the wave swept aboard. I was on lookout on the wing of the upper open bridge, took one look and damn near froze with fear. I managed to wrap my arms around the steel stanchion that was normally used to rig tarpaulin sunshades to and hung on for dear life. I was under a maelstrom of water for what seemed like an hour but must have been all of two minutes. I had on oilskins that were tied by cord at the waist and the air trapped inside helped to float me up to the top of the stanchion where a wire cable was threaded through eyes in the top of the stanchion. I emerged finally from the water and after choking and gasping for breath realized that I was suffering agony in both arms. On examination, both arms had wire marks carved in the flesh to the bone where I had been stopped by the cable from being flung by the wave into the sea. The ocean is a very harsh mistress. The damage to the ship was not too bad. Boats were smashed to kindling on the starboard side and most of the Carley life rafts were washed overboard. We bunkered at Halifax and topped up with water and stores.

We joined a large convoy out of Halifax and started the long journey over the Atlantic. Gale after gale greeted us as we plowed our way through the cold, wet weather. Life was miserable and submarine attacks were continuous. Some ships were lost, but memory fails me as to how many and who they were. Picking up survivors under conditions as severe as they were was a nightmare for the ocean escorts. Even then rescued men would be in severe danger of succumbing due to hypothermia. It was hell on earth to say the least. I was not invited to join the ship for her next voyage as I had had a disagreement with the Chief Officer, who wanted us to holystone the teak deck in a howling North Atlantic gale — this with ships being torpedoed all around us. I thought that it was the height of stupidity, as we could have been blown to hell at any time and told him so. He had us do sail-making with new tarpaulins as hatch covers instead. We were paid off in Glasgow and went home on leave. I heard later that she was lost with nearly all hands on her next voyage.

In early 1941, we joined the *S.S. Eskdalegate* in Leith and sailed to Cuba, Guantanamo Bay, for a cargo of brown sugar. What a hell ship. She was built around the turn of the century, and her so-called refrigeration was an icebox. All perishables were either eaten or rotted long before we reached the tropics. Every day during the trip south we had radio reports of ships being torpedoed but could do nothing to help. Life aboard this ship was a dreadful ordeal with fighting among the crew daily. The food was awful and the so-called fresh water was rancid. Some of the crew became so vicious that we had to sleep with one eye open and have a knife handy and ready for trouble. Conditions deteriorated the nearer we got to the equator.

Sanity was saved by our arrival in Cuba. When we arrived at Guantanamo Bay we took a taxi to Havana, where we proceeded to sample the local Cuba libres — what a night. The taxi was a revelation, as the owner had taken off the tires and set the taxi down on the railway line, which went all the way to Havana, noisy but fun.

We took off when loaded and sailed for Bermuda. This was my first time being served with liver (my favorite) with an iridescent sheen on it and a smell like an outdoor privy. Half the time we lived on toffee and melted brown sugar made from bags in the cargo that had broken open in the bad weather. One seaman was in so much agony from boils on his breasts that he had to make a brassiere from stiff canvas to keep his clothes from rubbing his wounds raw. We met up with the ocean convoy and while I recollect a great deal of depth charging by the escorts and some ships were torpedoed, I do not have a great deal of memory left of the final trip to our home port except that we were starving and covered with very bad boils. We were all glad to get away from that bucket of rust, as we called her.

Ship owners were notorious among seamen for being parsimonious and cutting costs wherever possible, usually to the seaman's detriment. Some, however, were so unscrupulous as to send ships to deep sea, knowing that they were fit only for coasting or the scrap yard; knowing also that the British Government had insured all ships for war risks. On our previous "scrap heap" they had complied with the very minimal requirements at best.

I joined the *S.S. Helmond* in Leith. This was a far better equipped ship with most of the original prewar crew still aboard, which helped to create a much more relaxed attitude in the forecastle. I was able to apply myself to my studies in relatively peaceful surroundings except for the occasional good natured ribbing about being so ambitious. We sailed part of the way in convoy then proceeded south alone to Jamaica to pick up a cargo of bauxite ore, which we delivered to the aluminum works at Burnt Island in Scotland.

We were loaded with the red bauxite in Kingston Harbor in Jamaica. The heat, with high humidity, and clouds of red dust made life in that tropical paradise pure hell for all of us. The dust got into everything including clothes and open sweating pores of the skin. Everything we ate tasted of the damned dust. On arriving home my mother was very irate when she discovered that her favorite dress was a slightly reddish hue, having been put in with my laundry for the sake of economy. Of the voyage itself, nothing comes to mind with the exception of continuous attack by submarines and the ocean escorts racing around the convoy dropping depth charges and of course the usual miserable North Atlantic winter weather.

We left the ship in dock in Grangemouth. In January 1942, after one week's leave I joined the *S.S. Harpalion* in Leith and discovered to my horror that she was loading lead ingots, cement, Bren gun carriers, heavy tanks, and ammunition. We were deeply disturbed to learn that we had orders to join a convoy and deliver our cargo to the port of Murmansk in northern Russia via Iceland; a heavy naval escort would accompany us.

Weather in the North Atlantic Ocean in winter was famous for its ferocity, and those of us who had sailed north of the Shetland Isles in the north of Scotland knew what we were in for weather wise. We did not realize what we would have to actually endure.

I had just come from a course at the British Naval Gunnery School, where we were drilled mercilessly by a crusty old CPO in loading, aiming, and firing the 4" ack-ack guns which were already installed on each ship's afterdeck. The ship's superstructure had to be specially strengthened to withstand both the recoil of the guns being fired continuously and the added weight of the gun itself together with ready ammunition lockers and the gunners serving them. We were taught how to lead the gun-sites ahead of the enemy diving aircraft in order to hopefully explode the shells so that the airplane would fly into the detonated shrapnel and be destroyed.

On checking the lifeboats for their state of readiness, we discovered that some moronic dockworker had stolen the hard chocolate from the lifeboats' survival stores. The water casks were mildewed and the ropes of the lifeboat falls were in dreadful shape. New block sheeves were fitted, and new rope boat falls were rigged. The oars had to be replaced, as the originals were split and dried out. None of the lifeboats were fitted with engines, which was just as well, as the water cooled type of engine used at that time would have exploded with the severe cold freezing temperature.

We left the port of Leith in Scotland in early January 1942 with a local pilot and a compass adjuster on board. Magnetic compasses and sextants were all we had to navigate with in those days; GPS and radar were not even dreamed of. Navigation in the bitter winters of the Arctic Seas is a complete nightmare due to heavy cloud, fog off the ice, and blinding snow storms. As we were circling the marks for the use by the compass adjuster who was busy changing the magnets in the compass binnacle at a fair speed the starboard anchor let go. The bosun and I were cleaning up the foredeck at that time took off, and we tried to let the officers on the bridge know what had happened. This proved impossible, as the noise generated by the thrashing anchor chain going overboard still attached to the 14-ton anchor drowned all speech. When the anchor hit the ocean floor, it dug in and caused the chain to rip the anchor winch and railings close by from their moorings and disappear overboard. On inspection, it was ascertained that the brake on the anchor winch had fractured and the mishap had followed. We were ordered to return to port for repairs. After the installation of the new anchor winch complete with new anchor and chain it was decided to fill the lower bow compartment with concrete, this to assist in reducing buckling of the bow plated when heavy ice was encountered. Days later we left port with a naval corvette as escort to join a convoy heading north, heavy fog set in, and before long we smashed into the escort and sustained more damage. Despite searching for a while in the thick fog we were unable to make contact with our escort. We were again ordered back to Leith independently for more welding repairs. We heard through the grapevine later that our naval escort had been cut almost in two and had sunk.

We felt deep sympathy for the grieving families left behind by this tragedy.

We left the port of Leith once again under naval escort for rendezvous with a convoy in the great naval base of Scapa Flow in the very north of Scotland. As the holding ground in Scapa Flow is well known to be rocky with poor holding ability and a major gale being expected the Captain ordered that both anchors be set.

Around midnight it was blowing a gale with wind speeds in excess of 105 miles per hour, and we were yawing all over the place. All at once both anchors wrenched loose and lost their grip on the rocky bottom and we took off rapidly downwind. The Captain ordered that both anchors be hauled aboard. The minute we got steam to the winches and the bosun started to heave in the starboard anchor, the drive shaft fractured. We drifted rapidly downwind and ended up broadside onto a deeply laden freighter. We smashed our way along his side, causing terrible damage to both ships; we then ended broadside under the bow of a big Norwegian ice breaker. As you know, the very high curved bow of the ice breaker is specially reinforced to enable her to batter her way through thick ice. The hydraulic ram fitted to her forefoot is a lethal weapon in a case like this. We were hammered for hours as the heavy seas and high winds smashed us up and down onto the ice breaker's reinforced bow. The damage thus created was horrendous. Come daylight, we could not believe that we had survived the beating. We found that the mainmast was in danger of breaking off and causing more damage, but fortunately the backstay broke and saved the day. All life rafts, carley floats, and lifeboats on the port side were smashed beyond repair, and the ship's side was battered in many places. A very large number of rivets were found missing along the ship's length, along with numerous fractured steel plates and badly dented ribs.

Around noon next day the weather had eased enough to allow two large deep sea tugs to come alongside and separate us from the clutches of the ice breaker. After the tug crew cut the errant anchor chains loose they towed us to a pier for examination of the damage. We were shocked to realize that in such a confined area of the anchorage where we were that there were over 100 ships of all types and sizes anchored there waiting to join convoys to various destinations.

We proceeded to Aberdeen in Scotland for repairs; from there we were ordered under naval escort to a rendezvous in the north of Scotland in Loch Ewe, there to join a convoy for the first leg of our voyage to Iceland. Two days out of Loch Ewe the German long range reconnaissance bombers found us and started transmitting our course and speed to the submarine wolf pack strung across our route and to the long-range bombers based in German-occupied Norway.

Twenty-four hours later the bottom started dropping out of the glass in the barometer, and we were hit with gales of 120 miles per hour. This produced mountainous bitterly cold seas, which charged aboard in solid masses. When so called daylight finally came, we discovered that we were on our own. No other ships were in sight. We battled on towards Iceland, at times having tremendous difficulty in maintaining steerage way into the heavy seas. Freighters in those days were usually underpowered for economic reasons. As the storm eased a German spy plane was glimpsed through the storm-wracked clouds. Whether he saw us or not we were fortunate enough to make our landfall in Iceland without being attacked.

The remaining seaworthy ships of the convoy from Loch Ewe that finally arrived in Iceland were remustered, and we left for the final leg of the voyage to Murmansk. This time we felt that we had a decent escort which was made up of cruisers, destroyers, and corvettes. Two days out of Iceland we were advised that there were a number of U-boat wolf packs strung across our route. Next day the glass in the barometer started dropping rapidly and a howling Arctic gale hit us with all its fury; it was so cold that ice started to form on the decks and lower rigging. Lifelines had been strung along the deck but were completely, useless as they were quickly plated with ice. All hands that could be spared were set chopping ice off the deck and gear. It became a never-ending grueling and dangerously brutal task as new ice was forming much quicker than we could break it up and shovel it overboard. We then started to realize that a major problem was developing as the ship was starting to lose stability due to the solid weight of the ice buildup. At one time she rolled over to 40 degrees as registered on the clinometers, we all thought that we had had it, but a tremendous wave hit us and helped the ship right herself. Everything that could move had done so, including, unfortunately, some of the heavy cargo. The Captain held the ship's head directly into the teeth of the weather long enough for us to open the main hatch and find the problem; a very large battle tank had broken loose and had smashed up Bren gun carriers and had damaged the plates of the hull. We started to try to attach chains to the big tank; this proved a vicious and agonizing business, as every time the ship rolled or rose to large waves the tank took off again and committed more mayhem. A check of the ship's hull revealed that severe damage had resulted to the ship's side plates and ribs. Since they did not appear to affect the ship's seaworthiness the engineers plugged the missing rivet holes.

Underway again, we were battling the waves of dive bombers, torpedo bombers, and U-boat torpedoes. The bombers came in wave after wave. The din of machine guns, big aircraft engines roaring flat out, heavy anti-aircraft guns hammering away, bombs exploding, and depth charges exploding nearby on an underwater contact by the escorting destroyers. The magnitude of sound created by this combination is extremely difficult to describe. Patches of Arctic fog started to drift in off the ice fields. We then had the added terror of the possibility of hitting an iceberg. All this time we were forcing our way through packed ice and very large growlers.

Conditions aboard ship were nightmarish, as ice had formed on the walls inside the accommodation due to condensation. This ended up nearly ten inches thick in the crew's quarters, which were located right up in the bow of the ship, and life was extremely miserable. Clothing was permanently wet with salt water, and we had no means of drying them. All hands were suffering from saltwater boils where heavy clothing rubbed exposed skin.

Another gale came at us, and come daylight, such as it was, we could see no sign of any other ships in the convoy. As we had been warned that the Germans had dispatched a trio of heavy-duty destroyers to intercept and destroy our convoy, the Captain made the decision to head as far north as we could go and hug the edge of the northern ice field.

We were hammering our way through heavy ice fields when we saw a war ship appear on the horizon. We thought that the Germans had found us, and we knew that we did not stand a chance of surviving an attack. Luckily it was one of our own destroyer escorts out scouring the area for the lost ships of the convoy. He then checked positions with us and agreed with the Captain's decision, but had to leave us immediately, as our cruiser escort had located the German destroyers and was in direct combat with them and needed the help of the destroyer's torpedo tubes to finish one of the enemy destroyers off.

We fought off numerous, vicious, and sustained bombing attacks with only superficial damage and made landfall at the entrance to the Kola Inlet. As we approached the entrance to the harbor a British cruiser signaled us to hang back and let him enter the port first. Our

Captain objected, and the Naval Commander aboard the cruiser gave us a direct order to desist or else! We did so with bad grace and, only as we circled around, did we see the reason for the cruiser commander's poor behavior — there was a hole big enough to drive a locomotive into the port-side of the cruiser, with bodies and bits of bodies washing in and out of the hole in her hull.

We learned later that the cruiser had fired her torpedoes at the German destroyer and that they had malfunctioned, due to the lubricant then being used and having gelled up with the severe low temperatures which existed at that time.

As we expected, the minute we berthed alongside the wharf and started to unload cargo, the air-raids recommenced with constant heavy bombing and machine gunning. As the nearest German airfields were only around 100 miles from us in enemy-occupied Norway, we knew what was coming. Our ship bore a charmed life while unloading; bombs were constantly dropping alongside the ship, they landed either in the water or on the quay where the cargo was being loaded directly onto flatbed railway cars by big, heavy women stevedores who yanked the winch steam valves wide open with dire consequences. One large battle tank reached the masthead and promptly broke loose and smashed its way back into the cargo hold. It was awe-inspiring to see the Russian gunners still firing at the aircraft as the warehouse roof they were firing from was collapsing under them. The noise and confusion was an absolute nightmare.

We were constantly running short of ammunition and had to beg the destroyer's Captain for supplies, and they responded magnificently. Between manning the guns and having to constantly splice cables for our lifting gear, which the Russian stevedores were using to unload the cargo, we were suffering badly from torn and bleeding hands, that together with the lack of sleep and bitter cold, took a tremendous toll on our physical ability to perform our work properly.

One of our sister ships was anchored far up the bay, having been badly damaged by the bombing, and was waiting for steel plates to make repairs. Every time steel arrived for them, the Navy commandeered the steel for repairs to the Naval Escort ships. Her crew members were nerve-wracked skeletons and desperate for food and to get home. We gave them all that we thought that we could spare, but that was so little that they took to visiting us and appropriated everything not nailed down. We had to mount an armed gangway squad to keep them from coming aboard. While we sympathized with their plight, we knew that we had to run the gauntlet of the return journey and would need everything we could conserve for ourselves.

During a lull in the bombing we went ashore to a field near the wharf to kick a football around. As we played some young Russian boys about ten years old approached and, as they seemed interested, we made gestures for them to join us and have fun. Ten minutes later a squad of Russian soldiers arrived and scolded the children, then escorted us back to the ship at bayonet point. After what we had gone through, we were all very much annoyed. Some idiot amongst us came up with the brilliant idea of us all getting shots of vodka, lining them up along the bar, then lighting them, a brilliant blue flame shot all over the bar; once again we were escorted back to the ship at bayonet point by the Russian soldiers.

The men in the engine and boiler rooms were magnificent. They deserved and had our deep and sincere admiration for their extreme fortitude in carrying on while all the action top-side was taking place. They knew that in the event of our being bombed or torpedoed that they stood very little chance of saving themselves from the horrors of being scalded to death with ruptured pipes from the high pressure steam boilers, or being trapped below and unable to get out before the ship sank. It is difficult to imagine the sheer gut-wrenching terror they felt each time another ship in the convoy was torpedoed or bombed, the noise of which is transmitted through the water and into the steel hull next to them. Sound, as you all know, appears to be magnified when traveling through water.

After nearly three weeks of this we were all moving around like zombies, as light at this time of year in high latitudes is almost twenty-four hours long with just a hint of twilight for a very short period. This of course meant continuous air attacks and worst of all no sleep except cat-naps fully clothed. We were very pleased to get our orders to join a convoy for home. Half a day out and the bombers found us again. They pounded hell out of us.

Next we ran into a major ice field loaded with large ice-bergs. We had just cleared the ice field when the first ship was torpedoed, then the next ship was hit; all the while the bombers were coming over us in waves. Our ship was hit in the stern with a string of bombs that lifted her out of the water. When she slewed out of line, we knew that we had had it. After a quick inspection we found that the rudder and stern gear had been blown off and we were taking in water at a fair rate. The Captain asked for a tow, but the Naval Escort Commander said no, and ordered us to abandon ship immediately, so that he could sink her and make sure that the Germans could not get tugs and possibly a salvage crew out to her. As we were only one hundred and twenty miles from the enemy on the North Cape of Norway, his decision made sense, but was a grim blow to us.

HMS Fury, a British destroyer, stood by us until we had gotten into the lifeboats and away from the sinking ship, which the German aircraft were still bombing and machine-gunning. Seemingly the German airmen had orders to destroy our crew as well as ships so that even if new ships were available there would be a shortage of ships' crews to man them. We were desperately trying to get clear of the ship as she was being wind-driven on top of us in the lifeboat at a great rate. With the heavy sea running, an over-loaded lifeboat and an exhausted crew, it was a monumental nightmare. A bomb dropped close by the lifeboat and that immediately galvanized us to su-perhuman effort and we pulled clear of the sinking ship.

We rigged a sea-anchor and used four oars to help keep the lifeboat's head into the sea. This was exceedingly difficult due to the overloading of the lifeboat.

The destroyer took off at high speed to rejoin the convoy escort after telling us he would come back for us as soon as he could. There is no way to describe the feeling of desolation that this created. We thought that we were being abandoned to the mercy of the Arctic Ocean. Conditions in the lifeboat were dreadful, as we were not only heavily overloaded, due to having twenty survivors from another sunken ship with us, but the other lifeboat had been destroyed by aircraft cannon fire. We were shipping water in the rough seas and had very little room between us to be able to move and bail out the slushing, icy bilge water.

The destroyer finally returned late that night, and the brutal task of getting injured and exhausted men out of the boat and onto the deck of the heaving war ship began. We all made it eventually, despite some odd instances of mindless panic. As you can imagine, space is at a premium on a "tin can," and *HMS Fury* was no exception. We ended up stinking with oil, sweat, and grease, lying in four inches of filthy water sloshing over the floor in the forward section of the destroyer, which at this time was doing twenty-one knots in the heavy seas in order to provide cover to the convoy from the German submarine wolf pack. We were advised that due to the number of U-boats present across our route, *HMS Fury* had to keep moving to provide a screen for the remaining ships of the convoy. I still have cold shivers at times when I think of those days. The destroyer's crew and the cooks were magnificent — corn beef sandwiches and hot cocoa were like manna from heaven to all of us. The commander of the convoy asked us if we wanted to transfer to the cruiser for the remainder of the trip to Iceland; we said thanks, but no thanks.

On arrival at Iceland we were transferred to an American troop ship called the *SS Borin Queen*. We were shunned by the U.S. soldiers as we came aboard. We were, of course in dreadful shape, with ragged and torn clothing and our unwashed bodies stinking. Our clothes were in tatters. We were gaunt with hunger and suffering from extreme fatigue. We all collapsed just as we were, in the iron bunks provided for the troops. Around five a.m. the next morning some moron blew reveille on a bugle, and immediately all hell broke loose. Nearly seventy pairs of heavy leather boots landed in the unfortunate man's direction. A pitched battle with the soldier MPs ensued. When the CO arrived he was told in no uncertain terms that we were Russian convoy ship survivors and were in no mood or condition to put up with this idiotic bugling. He said, "In that case I agree." No more any early morning noise.

The American soldiers responded whole-heartedly. They had been playing poker since leaving New York, and there was a large pot on the table. They immediately gathered up the cloth that the money was laid on and said, "Boys it is all yours, share it." We were astounded at this kind of generosity and really appreciated it. Furthermore, both soldiers and the crew got together and re-clothed every one of us, including shoes of some kind. We were all struck speechless at such a generous gesture.

It was a different story three weeks later when we arrived home and went down to the office of the shipping pool. The gentleman at the desk had the audacity to inform us in a gruff manner that all our wages and emoluments ceased at noon on the day that the ship was sunk. We found out that maritime law seconded the ship owners on that score. We also learned that any ship capable of getting to a convoy assembly point was covered for loss by war time government-backed insurance; consequently, some very poor specimens of ships were allowed to go to sea. The antagonism that this attitude generated among merchant seamen remains with many of us to this day. I have since heard that near the end of the war that someone in government had a change of heart, and wages, such as they were in those days, were paid until a man arrived home. I joined the *S.S. Harlem* as an Able Seaman. My determination to become a deck officer had started to become something of an obsession. I was low on cash, as usual, and had to buy all new gear and clothes, plus try to buy second hand books to replace those lost at sea with the ship. I remembered how the good-natured ribbing continued, but one of the deck officers helped me with my studies when we were on the graveyard watch together.

We were tramping coastwise all up and down the East Coast, picking up and dropping off all different types of cargo, including cement, coal, timber, etc. We had a great many vicious air raids to contend with, plus E boats and, worst of all, loose mines which had broken loose in bad weather and floated freely in the water of the inshore-restricted channels. When the convoy Commodore or the escorts signaled "free floating mines," the terror experienced was difficult to describe. Everyone knew the damage and devastation they created when they exploded alongside or underneath the ship. Usually, her back was broken immediately with a horrible death for all engineers and firemen stokers. Air attacks by Stuka dive-bombers and JU 88s were continuous. Fog and gales were a constant hazard to good station keeping and navigation. Lack of sleep was very debilitating and led to numerous problems.

On leaving the *S.S. Harlem* while walking around the docks in Leith I was very fortunate to meet a chief officer I had sailed under previously and in conversation he said they were desperately trying to find a second mate. I immediately asked him if he would consider giving me a chance. He said he would if the Captain agreed, but we had to sail within the hour. The Captain agreed under protest, so to speak. He said, "I will be watching you every minute." I thanked him and assured him I would not let either of them down. The ship was the *S.S. Corib*. The change to officer status is quite severe. To the officers you are uncouth and foul-mouthed and to the crew who seemed to be clairvoyant, I was an upstart getting way above my station in life.

It took a little time, but sheer determination, hard work, and being unafraid to ask questions plus the ability to lay down the law as I saw it, I was finally accepted all around. The fact that I had survived a sinking ship in the Arctic Ocean Convoy helped, plus my expertise with the Oerliken cannon, with which I was thoroughly familiar. The *S.S. Corib* was a very old and small general cargo coasting vessel and was engaged in the home trade, which meant tramping from port to port with mixed cargoes all up and down the east coast of the UK.

This entailed coastal convoys and proved to be a very nerve-wracking time. Winter in the North Sea is notorious for high gales and cold, wet mist or fog. The enemy aircraft used to hug the cloud cover prior to making their bombing run on the ships in the convoy, and the channels were usually narrow and often strewn with anti-ship mines. Outside the marked channels very little room was available to maneuver, especially when a ship was blown up and stopped ahead of you, thus leaving you to try to get around her and at the same time avoid collision with other ships in the convoy. Nighttime in fog was a horrendous experience, as we had to follow a little blue light hung on the stern of the ship ahead of us. Our ship being old, and the engine worn, the engineers had a major problem trying to give us exact propeller revolutions to maintain a constant speed. We were continuously running up on the ship ahead or falling behind and endangering the ships behind us. The naval escort captains were choleric in their endeavor to get us to keep good ship stations.

The enemy often mined the shipping channels and the mine-sweepers were constantly busy, but the bad weather often caused mines to break loose from the purposely sown minefields, and when a ship hit one, the force of the explosion usually destroyed the ship very quickly by breaking her back. In addition, the enemy E boats, which could do forty knots, would skulk around near a channel marking buoy to wait for the convoy to approach, and then start up engines and run at full speed between the double row of ships, all the time blasting away with machine guns and cannon fire, and throwing grenades on to the ships' decks as they thundered past. The confusion created by this type of attack was very great, as not only were we obliged to shoot back, we also had the problem of handling the ship in the confusion created. This type of attack usually happened on very dark nights.

Having been paid off the *S.S. Corib* and being on leave I was approached by my cousin and asked to be the best man at her wedding, to which I agreed readily. Margaret Mason was a bridesmaid and we were introduced. Bill, on seeing me looking at this good-looking young girl, told me, "Lay off, she is far too young for you." That did it; as we saw them off at the airport, I invited Margaret out to dinner and she accepted. From then on we met at odd occasions, then finally started to get seriously acquainted.

I joined the *S.S. Marquis* in Leith as Second Mate and was delighted to learn that she was going "foreign." My enthusiasm was dampened slightly when I discovered that we were the supply ship for both the garrison and the inhabitants of the Faeroe Islands, which were located north of the Shetland Islands and south of Iceland. We had numerous aircraft bombing attacks but seemed to bear a charmed life. On one occasion we were alongside the wharf in Toreshaven unloading cargo when the meteorologist sent a message to the Captain that an exceptionally bad storm was due within six hours. We ceased unloading, battened down the hatches, and made for a fiord down the coast that the Captain was familiar with. We sailed right to the head of the fiord and dropped not one but two anchors. When the storm peaked at 100 mph we realized that the anchors were not holding. We had to have the engines go slowly ahead while still drifting and maneuvering to stop the ship from crashing ashore. The wind was so fierce we could not breathe and ice pellets mixed with rocks and snow from the mountain were battering our faces and breaking the glass in the wheelhouse. The screeching of the gale in the confined area of the fiord was beyond description. By the time we drifted the length of the fiord we had to heave up the anchors one at a time, then steam back against the gale until we got to the top end of the fiord and drop both anchors again. This happened at least three times before the gale eased off a little. Everyone on deck suffered badly; cut hands and faces and the cold salt spray made life almost unbearable as it exacerbated the agony of the ragged wounds.

When the ship paid off in Leith and went to the shipyard for repairs, I reported to the Shipping Pool and was ordered to report to the Shipping Pool office in Cardiff in Wales. We were housed with a private family who had four officers billeted with them. All appeared to be senior officers with one gentleman, an Extra Master Mariner, who was the life of the group. After two or three weeks on standby without any shipboard duties, life in the family home seemed to become frigid. All talk ceased when I approached, and no one took any interest in talking to me. Two weeks of this was purgatory. I was young and out of my element in this exalted company anyway, but the atmosphere was to say the least dreadfully icy.

I applied two or three times to the shipping office to allow me to return to my home port, and they finally relented. I was home about ten days waiting for word to join another ship. The mail arrived one morning when a letter arrived for me, stamped from Cardiff. I was shocked to the core at the contents. The lady of the house apologized profusely for having treated me so poorly while I stayed in her home and explained that money had been going missing from a jar in the cupboard. It seemed that for years she had been in the habit of putting her paper money in a jam jar to pay for the weekly groceries. When it continued going missing after I left, they put ink on the bills and found that the Extra Master Mariner had been the culprit. He had an alcoholic habit that he needed to finance and he had told them that he thought I was the culprit. To my immature mind I was shocked to think that anyone would even dream that I would stoop to stealing money, and for a long time I was very bitter and resentful. Had they accused me I would have defended myself vigorously, but to be ostracized like that in a family home gave me a very bad feeling, which stayed with me for years to come.

The Shipping Pool office in Leith called to tell me to report and on going to the office I was dispatched to a ship docked in Glasgow. I asked if she was going foreign and they said yes. I agreed to sign on as Third Mate.

On arrival at the docks in Glasgow, I staggered down the pier with all my gear and when I found the ship, she was called the *Zamalek*. She appeared strange, very heavily armed and grim looking in her wartime paint with rust and buckled plates showing the results of lots of bad weather and worse. Workmen were everywhere. I found my cabin, dumped my gear, and went looking for someone in charge. The Chief engineer was talking to the yard foreman so I went back to my cabin, stripped and washed, and went back to the wardroom without my jacket, as it was very warm and I did wear a uniform shirt and tie with shoulder epaulettes. I was talking with a couple of the junior engineers and the first officer when a harsh voice at the door asked who I was and then was told to dress properly. My first introduction to Captain Morris was anything but cordial. Unfortunately, that situation did not change much in the time we sailed together. Fortunately, it was a personal thing between us and not professional.

I took a couple of days to absorb the fact that I had signed articles on a rescue ship which was fitted with a fully functional operating theatre, a Surgeon Naval Lieutenant, and six sick bay attendants to man it. In addition to the regular crew we had a yeoman of signals with three assistants, twenty-two naval gunners with a C.P.O., and lots of armament. I was very happy to see this. Our time was taken up in port taking on adequate stores, heavy weather gear, and lots of ammunition. One day the Captain came aboard and told us our next trip would be a convoy to Murmansk. Sheer, cold gut-wrenching terror gripped me, and I promptly packed my bags and headed for the dock gates. The Captain had not wasted time — he called the police at the dock gate who greeted me with, "Back to the ship, sir, or we will carry you." The Chief Officer asked what the hell I thought I was playing at. When I told him that I had had my fill of the Arctic Ocean and was a survivor from a ship sunk there, he was very understanding. The story got around ship quickly and attitudes changed for the better. Half my troubles were of my own making as I had always had a big mouth and said it like I saw it. Diplomacy was learned later!

The Chief Officer explained that we were to head for the *Gareloch* to practice with the lifeboats to ensure that the officers in charge and boat crew were trained to the highest efficiency. When I told him that I was an expert at handling small boats in the Thames River in London he was pleased. He knew that the currents on the river in a spring tide could hit 7 knots with heavy river traffic that stirred up quite a lot of surge.

The Captain did his best to create heavy weather conditions while we practiced lowering the boats and simulating rescue work, as small boat handling in a heavy sea is a highly dangerous business. A wooden boat crashing against a steel-hulled ship is a recipe for disaster. Injured men had to be helped aboard without causing more injuries while being transferred from boat to ship — all this while the convoy was being attacked by planes and submarines. Plus the continuous depth charging of enemy submarines by the convoy escorts and mostly in atrocious weather.

At times the rescue boats had to be left on their own to collect survivors from one stricken ship while the rescue ship herself went off to help others in distress. Often it was necessary to collect various boats together, rope them bow and stern and have the rescue launch head slowly into the waves in order to keep all the boats bow on to the waves. This could be extremely dangerous as with a heavy sea running the lines had to be long enough to provide a catenary or spring effect to avoid jerking the metal fixture out of the wood and at the same time be kept short enough to maintain control of the towed boats.

Some men were so badly injured that they had to be strapped in a steel stretcher and hoisted aboard the rescue ship by crane. Those who were capable climbed from the rescue launch onto the nets rigged over the ship's side. Great care had to be taken to avoid men being crushed between the rescue launch and the ship's steel side. In a couple of instances while going to rescue survivors under heavy bombing and torpedo attacks, some seamen survivors already aboard ship would charge to the lifeboats and had to be physically restrained as they were creating problems for the rescue launch's crew. Fortunately this did not happen too often. A machine gun fired over their heads got the message across. The problem was often exacerbated by the mixture of foreign languages spoken by the different nationalities of the crews from the sunken ships. The naval surgeon worked under extremely dangerous conditions in the operating theatre with the ship underway. Usually at full speed in heavy weather conditions, blood, water, excrement, and oil, etc., covering the deck where he was trying to operate, slipping and sliding was only part of his problem; however, the surgeon exhibited great skill in performing operations under these conditions. At times one of us was invited to help when all the medical corpsmen were fully occupied with bandaging other survivors. All in all, it was a fascinating experience. Simple language is inadequate to describe the conditions experienced by all the engine-room staff. The heat and the constant noise of moving machinery plus the continuous explosions of the heavy depth charges by the escort destroyers, together with the near misses of the heavy bombing raids, are all magnified by the water and the noise made by the multiple explosions resounding through the hull, made life sheer hell for all below the water line. Plus, they have no way of knowing what is going up on top. They live every minute with the knowledge that a torpedo could hit the ship and leave them scalded with high-pressure steam and with no opportunity or time to save themselves. To my mind they deserve every accolade known to man!

Unfortunately for the rank and file aboard ship, Maritime Law with its idiosyncrasies dictates that the crew sign on for each voyage. If the ship sinks for any reason, that voyage is deemed terminated at the particular time of sinking, with dire consequences for the crew as all wages and emoluments cease as of noon on the day of the ship sinking. This happened to many seamen in wartime, including the writer. The devastating effect that this had on all personnel was difficult to describe. The reaction when the survivors were so informed often with minimal courtesy was often violent. Wages, to say the least, were not far above subsistence level anyway and to lose everything one owned together with loss of wages was enough to generate very ill will among U. K. seaman in wartime.

In addition, merchant seamen in Great Britain were treated with contempt in many cases during wartime, as they were never in a uniform of any kind, officers excepted. People assumed that if you were not in uniform that you were a draft dodger or had a cushy job in a factory earning good money. What has never been pointed out to the populace in general is the fact that almost all food, munitions, planes, tanks, and soldiers were brought to Britain in ships manned by merchant seaman and officers. In addition, all invasions of offshore countries were transported in ships manned by merchant seamen. We were called noncombatants, but every seaman I ever met volunteered to man ships for the future invasion of the European continent and the majority of them were trained to handle all the guns fitted to the merchant ships by experienced Royal Naval Gunnery experts, the writer included.

In cases of a large convoy from the USA or Canada crossing the Atlantic Ocean, the Lieutenant Surgeon of the rescue ship had to act as a G.P. to all of the myriad crews aboard the various ships. This entailed lots of small boat work, often in very worst of bad weather.

Life was never dull aboard this type of ship, which was all on the small side with very low freeboard. This was to allow the easy rescue of men from the water and the boats. In addition, they had to have a good turn of speed and be fairly quick and easy to maneuver.

Many times we had to run at full speed through the ranks of ships with bombs falling on every side and submarines firing torpedoes at various ships, all this with heavy anti-aircraft guns going full bore. Our ship earned many compliments for the way she was handled under those conditions. Our arrival in Halifax, Nova Scotia, was always a wonderful time. The local people were extremely hospitable, and we were all guaranteed a home-cooked meal with a family ashore. In addition, deer and duck-hunting parties were laid on for us wherever we went. Nova Scotia was a relatively dry state liquor-wise, so we were doubly welcome when we took our own beverages with us. The Mounted Police were very understanding and allowed us a reasonable amount of alcohol for our own use while we were in port.

The purpose of the British Convoy rescue ships was

to save men from the ocean water when their ships were destroyed by the enemy.

The last three months of 1939 saw 126 British ships sunk due to enemy action, together with a very large portion of the crew. In 1940 a total of 640 ships were sunk due to a vast increase in enemy submarine activity, together with bombing by long-range bombers operating from captured airfields closer to the Atlantic Ocean.

The loss of ships, bad as it was, could be replaced by purchase abroad and new construction at home. The loss of experienced officers and crew were next to impossible to replace as the general war call-up of all able bodied men had taken the best of all available personnel. The pool of experienced officers and men at this time was seriously depleted, as the country as a whole was in the early process of recovering from a long period of economic stagnation. With the consequent loss of jobs, many experienced men had abandoned a career at sea. Due to the tremendous loss of lives the decision was made to purchase and or acquire ships capable of being converted to specialized personnel rescue ships.

Ships were to be selected with a gross tonnage of around 1,500 tons. This type of vessel was the kind employed in the general cargo coasting trade around the British Isles and the European continent. These ships though small were all low in the water at deck level; this was vital in getting men out of the water and from the small rescue boats. You must remember that most of the waterborne survivors were suffering from shock, hypothermia, and had ingested thick fuel oil into their lungs, this mixed with sea water. In the early stages, time being desperately short, these ships were quite basically fitted out and proved very inadequate to serve the needs of the survivors. Basic supplies were the order of the day, but as time and experience increased, a fully qualified surgeon and appropriate medical personnel, together with a well-stocked operating theatre and sick bay, were installed. A large contingent of naval gunners were put on board together with a 4" ack-ack gun and a Bofors cannon together with numerous banks of multiple Oerliken 20mm guns. These weapons were vital, as the ship had to have the ability to defend itself from aerial bombing attacks while carrying out rescue work away from the protection of the naval convoy escort group. This happened frequently.

It should be noted here that these ships having been designed for use in the coasting trade were subjected to tremendously adverse conditions when sailing in the vicious gales and mountainous seas in the Atlantic and Arctic Oceans. They were tossed around like corks in the storms and were often observed partly underwater at times. This made conditions on board completely and utterly miserable.

One wooden lifeboat was fitted with an engine, but invariably, due to bad weather conditions in the open ocean it gave us a great deal of trouble despite the expert and loving care bestowed on it by the ship's engineers. Boat work was carried out primarily with oars, and the breakage of these was very heavy. It should be noted here that the so-called lifeboats referred to are the old-fashioned clinker built heavy wooden type that had been the norm for many years. These boats were still lowered by means of ropes and pulleys. These were the cause of many problems due to the seizing up of the pulleys and the fouling of the associated rope falls as the boats were being lowered into the often heavy seas encountered in mid ocean and were exacerbated when operating in the ice choked Arctic environment.

The following is a story of one of those rescue ships. She was called the *S.S. Zamalek*, which I had the privilege of serving on for a number of voyages. These included crossing the Atlantic Ocean convoys to Halifax in Nova Scotia in Canada to Iceland and Murmansk in the Kola Inlet in Northern Russia. I was ordered by the shipping pool to join the ship in Glasgow in Scotland. My first impression on seeing the ship was shocking; I wondered what I had gotten myself into this time. Between battle damage and rust and with numerous ribs showing, which I learned later were caused by collision with heavy ice and with maneuvering alongside sinking ships during the rescue of her crew. When I learned that her next trip was back to Murmansk in North Russia, I was aghast as I had had the dreadful experience of being a survivor in a lifeboat from a ship sunk by bombers in the ice-choked waters of the Barents Sea on the way back from delivering cargo to Russia. After vigorously protesting about being forced to make the same trip again I was told in no uncertain terms what the consequences were if I did not complete my contract and make the voyage.

We spent the next two weeks in the *Gareloch*, practicing dropping the small boats into as rough water as we could find. Some RAF launches helped by making heavy waves as we were dropping the boats into the water. This helped us to simulate open ocean bad weather conditions.

Small boat handling in the open ocean is a major experience when coupled with picking exhausted and wounded men out of the water who were close to death due to heavy waterlogged clothing and suffering from hypothermia, etc., all the while the enemy submarines and heavy bombers were attacking the convoy.

The *SS Zamalek* was built in 1921 in the Clyde area and was owned by an Egyptian company called the Khedivial Mail Coy when she was acquired in 1940. *Zamalek* was probably the happiest ship I have ever had the privilege of serving on. Her crew were a dedicated group and were extremely efficient in carrying out open-ocean rescue work. Captain Morris was a superb ship handler and made a habit of telling each bridge officer, "Do not wait for me to get to the bridge, act immediately when an emergency occurs, get this ship where she is required." We not only picked up survivors from the sunken ships but pilots from downed aircraft. Our surgeon was kept busy at all times. To watch him operate on a badly wounded man in a heavy sea was an eye-opening experience. Many times he was forced to operate while our ship was being thrown about by heavy seas, and he had to do so with the floor of the operating theatre covered with a mixture of salt, water, blood, grease, and urine. When men died of wounds we sewed them up in canvas and buried them at sea. This was a terrifying experience as we knew that we could be torpedoed while stopped as we committed the body to the ocean.

With the increase in numbers of modern high-speed destroyers, updated with Huff-Duff and Asdic gear, the tide of war with the submarines was rapidly turning in our favor, and losses of ships and men were slowly tapering off. Cam ships with the convoys were another blessing. They had Hurricane fighters, which took off and made short work of the heavy bombers that had had the freedom to harass the ships until then. One of the rescue ship's jobs was to stand by the Cam ships while the planes took off, in case the pilot could not get enough speed for takeoff and tipped the plane over the side of the ship. Immediate pilot rescue was vital. In addition, if the plane ran short of fuel and had to ditch, we would break away from the convoy and search for the crew. This often proved highly dangerous and was never without the feeling of sheer terror being alone on the ocean without an escort and knowing that some submarine might have you in his sights ready to fire a torpedo into the hull.

Convoys ranged in number from a few ships to as many as a hundred ships. They were formed in columns with the escorting war ships ahead on each side and astern of the ships. Many of the ships were old with worn-out engines and some had mixed foreign crew. Some were very modern and were well-manned and efficiently sailed, as keeping station on the ships ahead, behind and on each side was a navigator's nightmare. Add to this the massed bombing attacks with submarines firing torpedoes and every ship blazing away with every gun they had, the escorts tearing around, the convoy dropping depth charges, and ships in the column in which ships ahead of them were damaged by bombs or torpedoes slowing down or sinking. The ships' Bridge Officers had a nightmare on their hands trying to avoid collision with other ships also trying to avoid striking sinking ships, or men and debris in the water from sunken ships ahead of them. The Commodore on his flagship would be signaling orders and instructions throughout the whole time. No ship except the designated rescue ship was allowed to stop to help any ship in trouble as it would have jeopardized the rest of the convoy. To sail through the wreckage of a sunken ship created mayhem with morale and went against all seamen's training and instincts. Enemy submarines were known to shelter under the convoy and travel at the same speed as the ships to try to elude the escorts or wait for an opportunity to speed ahead and let the convoy come up to them, then renew their attack. From the height of the ship's bridge on the Arctic convoys the water was so clear that the colored bands on the enemies' torpedoes could be seen as they approached. Most were set for the depth of heavily loaded ships, our ship drew only 17 feet at the bow, and we have known them to pass close underneath the bow while heading for another ship. The escorting destroyers and the submarines played a cat *and* mouse game when the submarines dived under the convoy. The destroyers' Captains had one major advantage on the submarines in knowing that the submarine had to come to the surface at some time to recharge batteries. While doing this even when they were fitted with snorkels they were still very vulnerable.

The camaraderie in our ship was amazing. I have never found this type of genuine personal concern for each other on any ship I have been on before or since. She was a happy ship regardless of the grim situations she was often in. Captain Morris had been awarded the D.S.O., which was almost unheard of in the Merchant Navy. He deserved that and more, as he was the Lynchpin that bound the whole crew together. His absolute trust in his officers was reciprocated wholeheartedly.

In addition, the *Zamalek* had the distinction of having picked up the most survivors of any rescue ship. A total of 665 men, all told.

In 1944, the Captain told me it was time I went to Nautical College and sat for my Foreign Going Certificate. I agreed, and he gave me a very good reference.

However, the Shipping Pool requested that I take a position as First Mate on a coasting ship to help out. I joined the "Hampshire Coast" as Chief Officer and left her in dry dock.

A quick call from the Shipping Pool had me joining the Captain and crew on a Naval Corvette. We were told we would be taking over a ship from another crew at sea. We did not expect what happened next. We made a rendezvous in the North Sea with a Royal Navy destroyer and a captured German merchant ship. Transferring crew in the North Sea was interesting, as was the fact that we were in direct contact with the German crew while we climbed aboard and took over after which the British sailors escorted the captured ship's crew back to the destroyer. The ship was owned by the captain and was called the *Ermland* and was very well equipped with very comfortable accommodations. The engineers in particular had a problem for a little while deciphering all the instructions, which were of course in German. We sailed her to Sunderland and were paid off there.

In early 1945, Margaret and I decided to get married and were deaf to all pleas to wait. The war at sea at this time was starting to ease off. We were so naive that we had no idea, nor did we give a thought to the economics or otherwise of our intentions. Life in those days was so different with the constant possibility of death or worse — something like dismemberment.

We lived with the premise "eat, drink and be merry, for tomorrow we will probably die." We had by this time fully accepted the fact that we were dead men just hanging on and waiting for the final blow.

As newlyweds we rented a room from my mother and moved in. To this day I will never understand how Margaret put up with me — we figure it took ten years for me to become civilized again and settle into a regular routine.

I joined a ship called the *S. S. Fenja* as Second Mate, but cannot recall the voyage or the final destination. On return to Great Britain and being discharged from the ship I applied to enter Leith Nautical College to study and sit for my Foreign-going Certificate. With minimal high school education I had my work cut out, and being adamantly determined to succeed I worked long, hard hours. I had to teach myself calculus from a book. Celestial navigation requires a first class knowledge of mathematics. I was adept in naval architecture, which helped. Maritime law was quite difficult for me to absorb but all in all my efforts at studying while at sea helped, as did the interest and help offered by a number of the Officers I had sailed under. In addition to the main exams, we had to have passing grades in lifeboat handling and first aid. Needless to say, I passed with honors in the physical aspects of the exam and failed in the written parts. I immediately applied to re-sit the exam in Glasgow two weeks later and was given the okay to do so. Monday morning I went back to the college to try to catch up, but the Extra Master who was teaching the new class told me to get lost as I was too dumb to make it! I repacked my briefcase and told the instructor a few facts of life, whacked his gut with my briefcase and went home, changed, and headed for a pub. My father put me on a train to Glasgow two weeks later, badly hungover, but very determined to succeed. The minute I sat down and was given the exam paper I was overjoyed to see that they looked very clear and straightforward. For four days I was supposed to sit — three hours in the morning and three hours in the afternoon. I actually only sat for one and a half hours at each section and wrote at a great pace. As I finished each section I checked it twice and then signaled the examiner that I was finished. He told me that it was impossible to complete the papers properly in that time that I had taken and that I was wasting my time and his. Fortunately I ignored his comments. I called him the following week and on hearing my name, he said, "You're through!" and slammed the telephone down. At first I was on a high, then the bottom fell out as I had grim doubts about what he meant. I was on edge for the next five days until the mail brought me my certificate. The war was rapidly coming to a close by then and as I was married to a lovely girl, I wanted to stay home. I requested to be discharged. On checking my records and my discharge certificates I realized that I first went to sea as a deck boy in 1935, and left with an Honorable Discharge as a Certified Deck Officer in 1946. The foregoing is accurate to the best of my knowledge, but some facts may be distorted by time, as my memory is not what it was, plus the fact that I entered a completely different way of life when I left the sea — one I am glad to say was very successful.

I was fortunate to have made friends with a gentleman who had started a mechanical engineering company in Edinburgh, and he offered me a position, albeit a lowly one.

From then on my life change drastically, but that is another story.

G. Graydon Service Medals

PHOTO GALLERY

George Graydon

George Graydon with U.K. Arctic Star

Russian Arctic Convoy 50th Anniversary

Ushakov Medal

*George and Louise with the Ushakov
Medal at the presentation ceremony*

*George receiving the Ushakov Medal from the Attache at the Russian
Embassy in Washington, D.C.—August 2014*

Embassy of the Russian Federation

6/7 Kensington Palace Gardens, London W8 4QP
Tel: (0207) 229-3628 Fax: (0207) 727-8625

Mr. George I. Graydon
3238 Ringwood Meadow
Sarasote Florida
34235 USA

...ember 2004

Dear Mr Graydon,

It is with great pleasure that I congratulate y... ...f of the Ambassador of the Russian Federation with the award that comes to you as recognition of your contribution to our common fight against fascism during the last war.

Let me remind you that the 50th Anniversary Commemorative Medal is given to you as a keepsake and can not be worn.

The Medal as well as the Certificate to it is being forwarded to you by the recorded mail together with this letter. Please, acknowledge its receipt.

Please find enclosed the translation into English of the Commemorative Medal Certificate.

With the best wishes to you and your kin,

Sincerely yours,

Pavel Andreev
Attaché

Arctic Convoy 50th Anniversary

George Graydon at Arctic Convoy Memorial, Loch Ewe

Rescue Launch picking up wounded seaman

Snow and ice covered the upper works of all ships.

Brave veterans of the Arctic Convoy, pictured 2014

Hero sailor frees chains, wires and bollards from the ice

*Frank Wilson was a seaman on the HMS Activity
and endured torpedo infested waters and sub zero
temperatures to assist Russian soldiers*

Those who took part in the British Arctic convoy ran a guntlet of U-boats and vicious weather conditions.

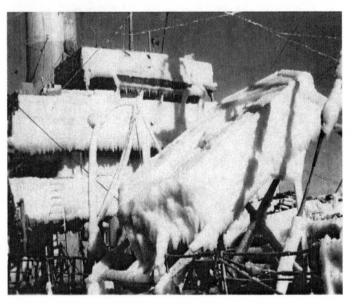

SS Zamalek covered in ice

SS Rescue ship SS Zamalek

One of 78 convoys that braved frozen seas to help win the war

Captain Morris DSO of SS Zamalek

The Rescue launch leaving SS Zamalek

Life Raft

Officers of the rescue ship SS Zamalek

SS Zamalek in the midst of an Atlantic storm

The deck officers of the rescue ship SS Zamalek

SS Zamalek coated with ice

George and Margaret Graydon married in February 1946.

LIFE AFTER LEAVING

My Career At Sea in 1946

In late June 1946, I started working with a mechanical contractor friend. My first job was to install the underground services for the aluminum houses being built all over Scotland by the Government; this was to offer accommodations for the working population of the U. K. The heavy bombing by the Germans had created a severe housing shortage throughout the country. I traveled all over Scotland with a crew of mechanics installing the underground services for the houses. The construction of aluminum houses also provided continuity of work for the aircraft industry. On completing the projects, I was asked to go to London with my family — my wife Margaret and my little daughter Wendy — to help the local manager there. On arrival in London, I was immediately sent to a project in Whitechurch in Surrey. We found accommodations in an old fourteenth century pub. Our bedrooms in the attic had a nine-inch slope to the floor, which were accessed by a very narrow circular staircase. The winter weather was very cold with frost, snow, and high winds. Linen sheets were the only type supplied. Margaret and I frequently sat in the old parlor, which had a tiny gas fire, and enjoyed a glass of wine. Occasionally we played a game of darts in the pub proper. Our landlady was a very thrifty person, and we discovered that any vegetables left on our plates were served the next day. We used to give Wendy pennies to play with, and she often hid them under the corner of the carpet. When she could not find them later on, she started to cry her heart out. I kept watch one night and caught the landlady lifting the carpet and pocketing the coins — that trick ceased right then. One evening while relaxing in the lounge Margaret and I were taken aback at some peculiar sounds coming from the dark spiral staircase — this was accompanied by a flickering light. An apparition suddenly appeared, and Margaret took off with a great scream of horror. It was the landlady's mother, who had no teeth, white hair flying in all directions, and clad in a bone-white nightgown holding the flickering candle. It took Margaret a long time to forgive me for laughing at her antics. With the project completed, we were moved to London and found accommodations in Acton, West London, where our younger daughter Carol was born. We carried out a great deal of restoration work on the many bomb-damaged buildings that were repairable — this entailed sheet, lead, and copper work. We fabricated new gargoyles from sheet lead. In warm weather it was quite comfortable, and the warmth made the lead much more malleable. The manager retired and I was given his job. I started to make a few changes and tried to make a more efficient operation. I introduced a system of making templates for repetitive work and intended to move as much work as possible into the warehouse under cover, as this would make for better supervision of the work and hopefully produce a superior product. This did not go well with the boss, who was a very conservative type.

After serious discussion and much rancorous talk, the boss brought in a man to replace me. I quit immediately.

I then drove to City Hall to sit the exams for the General Contractors license in my own name. Once I passed and obtained all the necessary licenses I started in business as Graydon & Coy in March 1949. Things were not easy, as all materials were in short supply and available good labor was hard to find. We slowly built a reputation for quality work and on-time completion, but were not doing as well financially as I had hoped, then I got a break. I managed to land a contract with a large brewing company called Charrington's, who owned a great many pubs scattered all over London. The contract called for complete maintenance. I started to feel as if I was living in my truck.

On getting home late one day, I was greeted with a panicked phone call from Margaret. She and the girls were stranded in a Lyon's tea shop downtown and due to the thick yellow pea soup-type fog could not see her way to get home. Having just been through that I knew how they felt. I found two heavy flashlights and a coil of rope and set off for town. The fog was created by a sea mist off the river and the sulfur put out by the millions of coal fires used for residential heating in the city. I was on my hands and knees most of the way and met numerous people trying to guide all kinds of vehicles down the road. On meeting the girls, I gave Margaret one flashlight and after tying the cord to the children's pram set off home. It was a nightmare as we were all coughing and sneezing and rubbing our eyes. I met a bus conductor head on at the edge of the sidewalk. He was trying to conduct a bus back to the garage. When we arrived home my knees and elbows were all raw and my dungarees were ripped at the knees. This situation was finally dealt with by the government, who demanded that only smokeless coal fuel be used in the city.

One day I had a call for the use of our very long extension ladder. As the truck was in use out of town, I strapped the ladder on to the box side car of my motorcycle and took off for the site. Negotiating around Marble Arch in the heart of the city created a major uproar. Motorists and pedestrians alike were aghast and their remarks were very uncomplimentary. Luckily, the policeman on traffic control was a good friend — we both belonged to the same motorcycle club and after a lecture he let me go on my way.

My father being out of work at that time asked me for employment. After much thought and against my better judgment, I employed him. Work overload and shortage of decent supervisory personnel forced me to put him in charge of a crew who were re-roofing a public house in Greenwich. After a frantic call for help from the pub manager I jumped into my truck and stormed down to the job-site. On arrival I could find no crew and the heavy rain was pouring into the pub, creating a terrific mess. I walked around the neighborhood until I located the crew, who were comfortably ensconced in a cafe drinking tea and listening to my father telling them how he would run the company if he owned it! I stood speechless for all of ten seconds, then exploded. I fired my father on the spot then stormed back to the pub, apologized to the manager, then climbed onto the roof and completed the job. The cleanup took quite a while.

Unfortunately the damage had been done and I lost the main contract.

I felt so devastated and betrayed that I took Margaret and the girls to the beach at Hastings in order to discuss and to get her agreement to do what I had in mind.

I proposed selling the business and emigrating to Montreal, Canada. Then I asked Margaret if she would be willing to return to stay with my parents in Edinburgh while I established myself in Canada. I explained that it might take two years to save enough money for their fares. After serious consideration she agreed. I had an uncle in Montreal with whom I met numerous times when our wartime leaves coincided in Edinburgh. We had become very good friends, and he invited me to stay with his family if I decided to emigrate. "Our home is your home" is how he put it.

Having been in Nova Scotia many times I was aware of the different way of life on the other side of the world, and I liked it.

Selling up was a traumatic experience. I remember particularly Wendy's three-wheeled bicycle; it was red with white-walled tires and had a step in back for Carol to stand on. The girls would go charging down the sidewalk laughing and waving to all their friends. It broke my heart to part with it, knowing how they felt.

When it came to selling the doll house that I had built for them, it brought back happy memories of the girls laughing and giggling while rearranging furniture.

There was one memory that I would rather forget — I had walked upstairs and heard the girls laughing merrily. Becoming curious, I walked into their room, which was three-stories up, and was just in time to catch Wendy before she fell out of the open window. She had climbed onto the roof of the doll house and was hanging out the window deeply engrossed in something going on in the garden below. Talk about a heart attack!

Margaret made all the arrangements to move to Edinburgh, organized the children's schooling, then found a job to help support them until I could manage to save their fares to Montreal.

I booked passage on an old passenger ship and left for Montreal in August 1952. I had previously advised my uncle and aunt of my time and date of arrival.

After a hectic, warm welcome in Montreal in August 1952, I headed for the licensing department, where I immediately ran into trouble. As a landed emigrant, the French Canadian Director demanded that I become an apprentice to a local tradesman. I was shocked and a wordy battle ensued. I told him in no uncertain language that my knowledge was way beyond the apprentice stage! He eventually agreed to allow me to sit the local examination. On presenting myself to the examiner I had a stroke of luck — he was a fellow Scot! Halfway through the examination he stopped me and said, "That is enough, I have not seen that kind of workmanship in many years — you have passed!"

Next day I walked into a local plumbing shop in Verdun and was employed immediately. I took a little while to familiarize myself with the different way of doing the work, but I learned quickly.

The truck driver took me to a very nice house and told me to install a hot water heating system to an extended patio. As there was a very nasty corner to get at, I decided to tin all the joints in that section of the copper piping prior to installing it. At that point a man with his arm in a sling tapped me on the shoulder and demanded to know what I was doing. I took a deep breath and told him that he had employed an expert to do the job and to kindly leave me alone to finish it, after which I would be pleased to hear any criticism. He stormed off, and when I finished the job and the truck driver picked me up he said, "Do you know who that gentleman is?" I said, "No, but he seemed pleased with the job." The driver said, "He owns our business." Ouch!

Our next job was to remove a faulty boiler section in a large commercial complex downtown. We rigged tackle and removed the old section and prepared the joints and gaskets for the new section. We broke for lunch and were sitting down eating when my helper let out a scream of terror, jumped up, and tore out of the building. On checking, we discovered that a very large rat had jumped down from the rafters onto his shoulders and took off with his sandwich. The next time I saw him he was in police uniform directing traffic!

I was on a rough construction site one day and sitting eating lunch when a French Canadian helper yelled at me, "Where is the toilet?" in French. I shrugged my shoulders and said, "Sorry, I do not speak French." He then swore at me at some length in French and said he hated these damned immigrants who came into his country and took all the good jobs. A guy near me stood up and in a broad Scottish voice said, "Sit down, you damn fool, you should never talk like that to a Scotsman!" The guy kept on, so I stood up, went to my bench, undid a six-foot length of galvanized pipe and swung it with everything I had. The guy, being over six feet tall, went down as if he had been pole-axed. He was way too big for me to tackle him head-on. Sandy, the Scotsman, said, "I do not think you have killed him, but he will not bother anyone for a while." Naturally, he and I became friends.

Next day, Sandy and I were chatting over lunch when we heard the most horrible screech of metal being torn apart. Sandy rushed outdoors and discovered some cement truck driver had just run into his brand new Hillman convertible car. All hell broke loose! The driver took quite a beating that day!

The following day being Friday, we were preparing to leave the site when Sandy asked me if I would like to spend the weekend with him and his family. He said, "I have a farm in Bedford and am building a new house. If you will help me with the building, I will provide food, etc." After some thought I agreed.

We bought a bottle of rye whiskey and took off for the country. Halfway down the road Sandy stopped the car, hopped out, and gave the tires a kick; when I asked him what the hell he was playing at, he laughed and said the damn car will not go any faster!

We were just finishing up one day after plastering the front room ceiling when Sandy noticed a tiny pebble stuck in the middle of a section of the new ceiling. As he went to remove it, I yelled, "no!" but he did cut it out of the ceiling and I took off like a bat out of hell, knowing what was coming. The whole section of new wet plaster broke loose and wrapped itself around his neck — scaffold boards and everything movable were catapulted out of the window! I stood well clear, laughing my head off — next day we had to redo the job!

We were called to an emergency late one night; the sewage in a restaurant had blocked. As it was three floors up, the damage was grim. On checking the basement, I realized that I had to get down in the manhole and loosen the bolts holding the cover of the backwater valve. Once the nuts were removed, I gingerly climbed out of the manhole and told my helper to stand well clear. The only thing holding the cover closed was an aged greasy gasket and natural suction. I stood well back and threw a brick directly at the cover. The gravity created by a column of filth, forty feet high, caused it to shoot up and hit the ceiling with force. Unfortunately, my helper, being the curious type, was standing looking down at the manhole. He ended up flat on his back covered in filth with a sanitary napkin draped from one ear! After completing a number of smaller-type jobs I needed a change and the opportunity to engage in something larger.

Meanwhile, Margaret and the girls arrived by boat in June 1953 and I was very glad to see them! We rented a house close to my uncle and started to settle in. The girls seemed to enjoy the change in this new way of living and soon made many friends. We started camping at Lake Meacham, in the northern part of New York State, and enjoyed it immensely. The girls also enjoyed meeting Santa Claus at his home in North Pole, New York.

Sandy asked us to the farm for the weekend and to enjoy a barbeque. While there, he asked me to assist in collecting the hay, which had been cut and bundled in one hundred pound bales. He asked me to drive the rig, which consisted of the tractor, a trailer, and a special rig which picked up the bales and threw them onto the truck bed. Quite a complicated set-up. Not too sure of what I was doing, I started slowly and steadily, got faster and faster, not realizing that Sandy, who was in the truck bed stacking the bales, could not keep up and was being battered by one hundred pound bales of hay. When I finally saw what was happening I was convulsed with laughter and took off for the house at a fast clip, knowing the violent reaction my antics had created. I was not invited to do that again.

I had acquired an old Dodge car. After patching, welding, and renewing brake pads and crawling around underneath, I had had enough. We all jumped in the car and went around the used car lots. I was driving around with the car salesman beside me and I was telling him how much I liked this old car and would be sorry to part with it, when my daughter Carol leaned over the back seat and in a delightfully sweet voice said to the salesman, "My father had such trouble with this car and will be glad to get rid of it." The salesman and I exchanged glances, and I promptly turned the car around and dropped him off, then told Margaret and the children to stay home while I went looking for another car alone.

On leaving late one Friday night to go camping, we decided that we had better find a closer campsite. We pulled into a site on the Richeleau River and as we made camp noticed another couple, Roy and Pearl MacLean, with their two children, who were about the same age as Wendy and Carol. They owned a very good looking trailer and I was very interested and asked him how it worked. This started a friendship which still lasts today.

I walked into a large shop one day looking for a change of work and was asked what my capabilities were. As ever, and, as bold as brass, I said, "You name it and I can do it." After discussing among themselves, the superintendent said we need a project manager to supervise construction of a number of D.E.W. campsites in Northern Canada. This would entail working seven days a week and twelve hour days — all work would be in the pristine bush and would entail all men and equipment being flown in and out by bush plane.

Once we had agreed salary and expenses I set to work. We cut up a small front-end loader that could fit in the plane and which could then be put together and re-welded on site.

We went by train to St. Isles on the lower St. Lawrence River, where we loaded the gear and six lumberjacks onto a truck and took off for Magpie Lake to board the float plane that was to fly us to the site.

Once the plane was loaded the pilot, having warmed the engine and performed his check list, took off down the lake and as he turned into the wind the engine started to misfire and sputter. The pilot then calmly told everyone not to worry as that happens frequently. He insisted that we all strap ourselves in securely. We took off the second time without incident, but the minute the float plane broke loose from the water and started to gain altitude, the pilot put her into a steep climb. The next thing I knew was that none of the seats had been bolted down and we all ended up in the tail of the plane, with seats and gear on top of us! Our pilot thought that this was hilarious. After a great deal of cursing and sorting out we resumed some kind of seating, vowing to deal with the pilot later. Because of various delays which made us late arriving at the lake in the dark, the upshot being that I had to open the cockpit door, hold it against the fierce slipstream, then stand on the float and shine a flashlight on the water surface to let the pilot see to land the float plane on the water. As you can imagine, both water and wind were bitterly cold and I was thoroughly soaked and miserable. Once we unloaded the plane and brought out our sleeping bags we found sheltered spots and turned in. We were completely exhausted. Next day the lumberjacks got busy building shelters. These were constructed of logs, trimmed and notched with a sheet plywood door and floor. The roof was canvas with an extra fly sheet. Heating consisted of a fifty gallon-drum with the head knocked off and burned logs — crude but effective.

The living quarters had to be built three miles away from the actual work site in case of a forest fire breaking out.

Two thirds of the way through the job we got instructions to prepare a landing field which could accommodate larger aircraft with larger loads. We had to build a road through "muskeg" for three miles in order to separate the fuel tanks from the vicinity of all habitable accommodations. We had to have a large quantity of trimmed logs cut and which we used to sink into the "muskeg" and form a corduroy road to lay the fuel pipe on. Let me tell you, Canadian mosquitoes are the largest and most vicious I have ever encountered! Every time we dumped a log, large clouds of angry insects swarmed up and bit the hell out of us. The weather deteriorated with ice and snow driving in. One day our dear "friend" the float plane pilot came in on skis. He was late and had to stay the night; to us this was perfect! To make matters worse, the idiot kept laughing because he had a two-inch thick goose-down filled sleeping bag. We, of course, had been provided with the cheapest sleeping bags available. When everyone settled down for the night three of us crept into the pilot's cabin, stoked his fire up with wood and tied the door open. I ran my finger down the canvas fly sheet that covered his roof and stopped right over his beard. Come morning his howls awakened the camp! His beard was frozen to his sleeping bag and his flying boots were frozen to the floor. When he was finally freed and came to see us, we asked him how he enjoyed payback! You can imagine the language used.

We had a major fire break out at the site, and it created a dreadful situation with two men trapped on-site. The bush pilot volunteered to try to get the men out but needed help, so he and I set out. The place was a nightmare of flaming wood and oil drums bursting and oxygen tanks exploding. We could see the men in the lake and signaled them to be ready for pick up. On getting them aboard the pilot said I cannot get off with this load. He said, "There is only one way, George, you tie us to the wharf, then stand on the float with the fire axe and when I gun the engine to maximum speed, chop the line and jump in! We did and the plane took off through the flames at the end of the lake, the floats touched the tops of the trees, but we kept going. That memory stayed with us for some time.

With the job successfully completed, I was given a job at the new Kraft Foods building on Cote-de-Neigh. My first job was welding the sheet lead that covered walls, ceiling, and floor of an x-ray room. Everybody wanted to know how it was done. This entailed lots of lead piping and specially treated glass piping for use with high acidic compounds. Lead-work was my forte and I received many accolades for it, but when I started on glass piping, which I had to cut and fit in very precise measurements, I had numerous visitors and requests for information.

I was welding a large number of copper pipes one night that were located on a large grid forty feet above the floor. Suddenly my eyes started to water badly and sting; next I started choking and gagging. I crawled along the pipework to the ladder and slowly slid to the floor, where I collapsed. Suddenly I felt myself being dragged along the floor and out into the fresh air. When I had recovered a little, I asked what the hell had happened and was told a crew with gas masks on had come into the room and opened up an ammonia tank to clean it. Not being aware that I was working above their heads, they had gone for a break. Fortunately, one of our people had come to borrow a tool from me and had donned a mask and dragged me outside.

With the Kraft Food project completed, there was a temporary lull in work, so I went looking. This was in early 1957.

I met a friend who was the general superintendent at a place called Tweddle Ltd. I was hired next day.

After completing a number of mundane types of jobs, the boss's son called me into his office and told me, as his father the owner was ill, he was taking control of the company. He then invited me to spend the weekend at his farm in the Laurentian Mountains. I accepted; he then told me that he was a ham radio operator and would I help him build a radio tower. This required welding pipes and fitting a counterbalance, so I agreed, having figured that he was up to something that might affect my future — "It certainly did" — his name was Don Storey.

I had heard through the grapevine that he was a character. We climbed into his car and took off for a restaurant called Ruby Fu's. When he ordered dinner, I requested a different type of soup and was greeted with a surly lecture and told to go with what he had ordered! I did not agree. Unfortunately for Don we had been drinking heavily at the bar prior to dinner. We got into his car, which I was driving, and I took off at high speed. I was in a very bad humor and when Don reached over and tampered with the gear lever — I lost it! I cursed him roundly, then drove my elbow into his throat. We went through the toll booth at one hundred miles per hour. I had the window open and fired the coins into the basket — then all hell broke loose — sirens going, lights flashing, and

Don sitting holding his throat. We arrived at the cottage, with Don apologizing — I swore at him and stormed off to bed. The following morning I accepted his apology and went to work on his antenna. As I was preparing to weld in a sea of tall African grass, I wet down the area around the oxygen and acetylene bottles, then I brought up from the lake a five-gallon drum of cold lake water. I gave Don very strict instructions to watch my back and extinguish any sparks that were created with the welding. I was happily working away, when suddenly my rear felt uncomfortably hot, and when I turned around and took off my goggles there was no Don and the grass all around me was on fire! I dumped the five gallons of water, raced down to the lake for more, and on struggling back up the hill I noticed that the front door of the house was open with voices and music blaring! I tore into the house and found Don lying on the floor in front of the TV with a glass of red wine in his hand. Well, being a man of action, I dumped the whole five gallons of cold lake water over "my friend," called him every foul name I could think of, then raced up and down and eventually put the fire out. Naturally we had a few words and I told him in no uncertain terms what would happen to him if he ever tried anything like that with me again. I started to get the impression that he was used to getting his own way and, while he was a brilliant engineer, he was also a brilliant financier and taught me a great deal about many things. I will be forever grateful for his advice and friendship.

Several weeks later Don called me into his office and

told me he needed a manager for a number of projects in Newfoundland and asked if I would be interested. After we negotiated terms I agreed. He then told me that before I went to Newfoundland he wanted me to finish a major job in Northern Labrador. He said that his superintendent Sam had been badly dealt with by the crew of mechanics that he had working there and that he had to be brought home. I agreed very reluctantly. I then told Margaret and the children what I had agreed to. They knew that I was taking the risk in order to earn the extra money I could make working in the bush seven days a week. I collected Arctic Gear and flew to the job site, which was called Knob Lake. To digress a moment, let me explain why a whole new town was being built in the wilderness. This was to accommodate the many people involved in the giant mining complex, which was discovered by a bush pilot shortly after the finish of WWII. As he was flying south from Hudson Bay his magnetic compass went haywire and finally steadied down. After turning around and flying over a cross-section of the area and being pretty intelligent, he reported his findings to his employer, who then sent in geologists who found vast quantities of high-grade iron ore, only nine feet below the surface.

A railway line was built through six hundred miles of *tundra,* solid rock, etc., plus a first class runway for large aircraft, and accommodations for five thousand miners and housing for executives with family, plus a Hudson Bay Store and a hotel.

On arriving at the site and talking to the manager, I was given the sad tale of Sam's problems. It appeared that the mechanics had gotten out of hand and Sam could not control them. Some of their tricks were diabolical. They had opened the door of his room, urinated on his steam radiator, then run a hose in and let the water freeze on the floor. Breakfast was at six a.m., so on finishing we all went out to the truck, which would take the mechanics to various parts of the project. The front cab was jammed with men and I knew that this was it! I ordered all but the driver out of the cab and when nobody moved, I did. I pitched the first guy bodily into the snow and in so do-ing, performed a dirty trick on him that I had learned in the Judo school in Montreal. Then did the same with two others. When the shock wore off they started to come for me, and I stopped them cold when I told them I was a "black-belt" and would have no mercy on any individual who attacked me. The moans and groans of the other two idiots convinced them that I meant business! The General Superintendent came over and said, "What the hell did you do to get that mob working?" I just grinned and said, "I talked nicely to them." He went off with a big grin on his face.

Four days later after checking the work site I called Don in Montreal and told him to send me thirty-five airline tickets by courier. He had an immediate fit and started to ask questions. I said, "That is enough — send thirty-five tickets, or one!" He said, "Who is the one for?" I said, "For me." He finally agreed, but before he sent them Don called the Superintendent and asked what was I doing. He told Don do not argue, just send the tickets! I understand he told Don that he had witnessed the whole episode with my men and told Don to give George anything he wants as he was delighted that my men were now working properly. There were sixty-five men on site when I arrived. After I had shipped the worst of them home, the remaining thirty men did more work than the original sixty-five. Don arrived on site a week later, and I asked what the hell he was up to. I said, "You have given me a job to do and you are now questioning my methods?" He apologized and said he was just there to help.

One day I sent a mechanic to tighten a small leaking half-inch-high pressure steam valve in a manhole. I went to see what was holding him up. Just as I dropped down the manhole, I found him with a two-foot wrench, tightening the valve! This size wrench was far too large for the job. The valve immediately cracked and high-pressure steam filled the manhole. I tore the wrench out of his hand and chased the damn fool down the street, threatening to kill him for his stupidity. My friend Lorenzo, an electrical engineer doing site work, told me later that he had stopped in amazement when this maniac with the wrench and enveloped in a cloud of steam appeared storming down the road, screaming obscenities at the mechanic. Lorenzo and I are still the very best of friends today and often reminisce and have a good laugh about the incident.

When the job was completed, I returned to Montreal. We took two weeks off. Visited with Roy and Pearl and had a great time. We next went down to spend time with Sandy and Diane at their farm. From there we visited with my sister, Patricia, who was in charge of a halfway house in Montreal, where she mothered and cared for sick Inuit Eskimo children. We were fascinated by the children's way of life, their outlook, and the way they dealt with the elements of their area. We noticed them sweating at 40 degrees Fahrenheit in Montreal. Pat had a wonderful collection of carved stone-work, which the grateful Eskimo families had given her in appreciation for caring for and nursing their children back to good health. Pat gave me a beautiful carved-stone set of chessmen, together with a seal-skin chessboard.

In Montreal we packed all our furniture for transmission to St. John's in Newfoundland by boat. With the car serviced, etc., we took off for Sydney, in Nova Scotia, where we would board the ferry for the trip across the Straits to Port Au Basque in Newfoundland.

After a long and tedious journey, we arrived in Sidney. When we boarded the ferry we found the overnight cabins quite sparse, but enjoyed the adequate hot water showers. After a stormy night passage we arrived in Port Au Basque, the westerly terminal of Newfoundland. With the car unloaded from the ship and filled with gas we set off for Cornerbrook, a town about one hundred and twenty miles away. After hammering along a very rough track for a while I was repeatedly asked by my children, "Where is the road?" I came up with a reply indicating that maybe they were just preparing the roadbed for final topping. The track consisted of large chunks of rock filled in with gravel. We bounced from one chunk to another, all the while being enveloped in a cloud of thick dust. On arrival in Cornerbrook we were greeted with a paved road, "Heaven!" We set off after two days' rest and immediately after leaving town limits the road resumed its track-like conditions with the thick dust. After bouncing around for a few days we were fortunate to find some very nice bed and breakfast homes, with most hospitable people. We finally came to the crossing of the roaring, flood-swollen "Exploits River." When our turn came, we were shocked at the dilapidated condition of the so-called raft ferry. We were concerned about being swept away downstream. On reaching the other shore I was stunned to see a wicked slope, coated with thick soft red mud, which meant poor traction for the car wheels. Having no option I told all aboard to hunker down, hang on, and pray. I gunned the motor and slowly fought my way to the top of the hill, where we all said a silent prayer.

Our next stop was at a village called "Come By Chance," where we had to board the famous narrow gauge Newfoundland Railway flatcar.

Unfortunately there was quite a crowd of vehicles waiting, so we booked our space on the flatcar for our vehicle and seating space for us. We found a house with rooms to rent and piled in. The landlord showed us our rooms, which looked nice and clean, then there was a chorus, "Where is the bathroom?" He politely showed us an empty room and told us that this was his next project!

He then took us downstairs, opened the back door, and pointed down the garden where we would find a "three-holer." We all shot off down the wet, muddy path in the pouring rain. The next thing I knew I was lying on my back in a muddy pool, clutching my throat where I had been trapped by a clothesline installed by the landlady the previous day. Needless to say, I was elected "comedian-of-the-day" by my daughters. The language was colorful to say the least! Carol was fascinated by the coal oil lamps used in the house and was shocked because there was no electricity.

Next day we had a stroke of luck — the guy ahead of us had a trailer which proved too long for the space available on the flatcar, so we moved on board.

There is a tale widely spoken about the famous Newfoundland Narrow-Gauge Railway that you can jump off the train at the front, catch a fish or pick a flower and jump back on at the end of the train. I must admit I do not think that it ever exceeded twenty miles per hour. After checking the car on arrival in St. John's it was very apparent that the damage sustained by the trip was so extensive that we needed to buy a new car.

On arrival in St. John's we booked into an old hotel. After dinner we went to the lounge and two delightful elderly ladies struck up a conversation with the girls. When the girls were offered sweets by the ladies they were thanked with glee. A short while later both girls were seen holding their mouths and had tears in their eyes. I diplomatically advised Margaret of the situation and they took off for the restrooms. On their return, I learned that each had been given a raw ginger chocolate covered sweet, which they both hated. The hotel had an offensive smell of old, stale cabbage, so we moved out and rented a home from a very nice fellow called Bob Lynch, who proved to be very knowledgeable about Newfoundland's history. I spent many happy hours listening to his tales. I had read many of a fellow Newfoundlander's books, and we both commented on his book called *The Boat That Would Not Float*.

After settling in, a fellow called Cliff Reid applied for the site foreman's job. He proved to be a great asset to the projects. After reading the specifications for the project for the third time I realized that we had a major problem on our hands. The City was supplied with fresh water by gravity from a lake three miles away and over a thousand feet above the city. This created great water pressure, but we discovered that the fourteen-inch supply pipe had been installed in 1914 and all the shutoff valves had since jammed in the open position and were now inoperable. I played hell with Don, over the phone, for not telling me about this, prior to me leaving Montreal, where I could have learned about the special technique and operation of the equipment required to carry out the branch connection to the water pipe for supply to our project. On surveying the route and the existing conditions I realized that we were in a very dangerous position. One wrong move and we could have emptied the huge lake into the town with disastrous results. Once the hole was dug all around the existing pipe, we had to bolt on a two-part cast iron sleeve with a built-in flange. We had to caulk it with oakum, then pour hot lead into the joint and hammer it firmly to get a watertight joint. This was no mean task due to the heavy weight of all components. We started fitting the joint, and when it came to pouring hot lead into the joint, steam flared out of the oakum and the mechanic doing the job jumped out of the hole in panic and ran off. I jumped into the hole immediately, as it was vital to maintain continuity of pouring the hot lead, and completed the job. I then positioned Cliff and two mechanics one hundred feet away from me, and uphill well above the manhole, with instructions on what to do if anything went wrong. I started drilling very cautiously, and slowly felt the cutter chewing away at the pipe. After what seemed like an eternity I felt the cutter break into the main water pipe. I then had to slowly withdraw the cutter, extract the section we had cut out, then close the new valve and withdraw the machine. With a feeling of great relief I jumped out of the manhole, soaked in sweat, to be greeted by a large crowd of well-wishers. When I called Don to report success his first words were, "Get the rig back onto the plane, as the hire costs are running up." My words to him were strong and extremely forceful. We had a call about trouble at the submarine cable station which was located on the north coast, so Cliff and I took off in the station wagon. As the Canadian government at that time was in the process of building the Trans-Canada Highway across Newfoundland, we proposed to try to use it. As usual, it had been raining for weeks. We had made about one hundred and fifty miles from St. John's when the car started slowing down. I said to Cliff, who was driving, "Get a move-on, we do not have time to play around." He said, "My foot is flat on the floor." On winding down the window we discovered that we were sinking into a morass of red mud. We spotted a light flashing and blew the horn. Sometime later a big Cat bulldozer appeared out of the rain; he was part of the crew building the new highway. He had been forced by nature to visit the privy and spotted our headlights. The driver yelled for one of us to get out of the car and hook on a chain he had attached to the front of the bulldozer shovel. We made the connection and returned to the car through the window covered in red mud, soaking wet, and shivering with the cold. The bulldozer yanked us out of the mudslide and towed us to the campsite, where we dried out and spent the rest of the night with them, then we carried on to the site, effected the repairs, and returned to St. John's.

We moved into a delightful, second-floor apartment in St. John's to be near the schools for the girls. At school they made friends with a couple of girls whose father was an avid fisherman. He invited me to go fishing with him and I really enjoyed myself. One day we were fishing on opposite sides of this large lake when I heard a tremendous uproar. I dropped everything and struggled over the rough lakeside to help him. When I saw the situation he was in I sat down on the lakeside and was convulsed with laughter. Dick had a creel full of fish on his shoulder, a rod in his hand with a fish on it, and a muskrat with its teeth buried in his rubber boot. In struggling to shake off the muskrat, he would drop into a hole in the lake bottom and come up shaking his head, spitting out freezing lake water and cursing to beat the band.

We had a great social life here as Margaret had transferred her membership in the Montreal Sorority of Beta Sigma Phi to the one in St. John's. We were invited to a barbeque on the beach at Conception Bay, where we watched some large whales drive the capelin onto the beach in large quantities. Once that stopped, we had built a fire of beach driftwood and were then shown how to shovel the fish onto the grate installed above the fire — they were delicious. Mrs. Casey Brown played the ukulele and sang. Mr. Casey Brown was the comedian. He tried to get people to go swimming and when all refused, took bets on the fact that he would. He disappeared, then turned up a few minutes later clad in an RAF survival suit and dove in!

I was walking down to the job site one day and was accosted by a panhandler who asked me for a dollar and a quarter. I was interested in that amount and when I asked "why" he said, "for a bottle of wine, you damned fool." I laughed and walked on. We were collecting more contracts, and I had to adapt our station wagon to deal with the wild conditions of the interior of the country. We welded gusset plates to the corners of the frame, then a sheet of boiler plate under the sump. We then equipped the wagon with two good sleeping bags, fishing equipment, rope and chain-falls, plus a complete second spare wheel, two five-gallon cans of gasoline, lube oil, etc., and a large quantity of canned food. We picked up a contract for a new school in Cornerbrook. I flew there, leaving Cliff in charge of the main custom house project in St. John's.

We were awarded a contract for the new submarine cable station located on the North Shore. This proved to be a very interesting project. This was where the cable from Europe was brought to this point by the British Cable ship that had installed the line deep in the Atlantic Ocean, all the way from the shores of Europe to the submarine cable station on the north coast of Newfoundland.

We held a great party at our house and when our guests arrived the male contingent agreed to shovel the driveway, as it was snowing heavily and they wanted to be able to drive out and get home. The party ended quite late and when the guests went to drive their cars they discovered that some wretch in a Volkswagen had parked across our driveway entrance. Our guests being in a jovial mood suggested that we lift the Volkswagen and park it on top of the big snow bank and let the vehicle's driver worry about getting it down in the morning. This was duly done and all our friends left for home in good humor.

About a week later a vicious blizzard blew in with high winds and heavy snow, it continued for two days, and we were all snow bound. When the blizzard eased, I tried to open the front door and could not move it. I finally opened the top half of our bedroom window and found the snow was right up to the second floor window that I was standing at. I persuaded my girls to lend me their sled and saying "I will see you later," shot out of the window on the toboggan and fought my way to the site. I was marooned on site for two days before help arrived, but I felt good as I had arrived in time to minimize the amount of damage to the jobsite.

Moose and deer hunting were favored by the populace, as they provided good nutritional food. Personally I loved fishing, especially in the interior of the country as it was impossible to access the remote lakes without heavy gear and very few of the local people could do so. This made sure that most of the lakes we fished in were pristine and the fish were not used to artificial lures. The trout we caught were a cross-breed with salmon and had pink flesh that had a wonderful flavor. Margaret used to package them in ocean salt water and drop them in the freezer. When thawed and cooked they tasted as if caught that day. If we saw one person fishing on a lake we were preparing to fish on, we would pack up and go elsewhere. Despite perpetual rain, Dick being a superb woodsman was able to dig out kindling from the forest floor and get a decent fire going quickly. Fish caught and cooked that way were scrumptious and fit for a king's plate. While walking downtown one Sunday morning a station wagon passed me with wall-to-wall children's faces showing at every window. As it looked like Cliff driving, I called him in next day and asked him if it was he I had seen. He said, "Yes, I was ordered to take all twenty three children out of the house and stay away for some time." On getting my breathing under control I said, "You did say twenty three?" He answered, "Yes — there were twelve of mine and eleven of my sister's and she was at home with the birth of my sister's twelfth child!"

One day I was invited to the Naval Officer's Club at the Crow's Nest for a ceremonial dinner. "Surprise!" The entrée turned out to be Seal Flipper for the main course. After copious amounts of whisky I tackled it and the meat turned out to have a very fishy, gamey taste — definitely I decided that it required a more sophisticated palate. After nearly three years the projects started to dry up, and it was decided to shut down and have me return to Montreal. We sold off everything and flew back to Montreal. We had to stop in Gander due to engine trouble with the plane, and the girls got a taste of army life. We were housed overnight in the old army barracks and had to sleep in tiered bunks with thin mattresses and a naked light bulb hanging by a cord. What a shock for them.

On starting back in the main office in Montreal, I had completed a couple of projects when Don approached me with a proposition. If I would throw in the bonus I had made from the profits we had made in Newfoundland, he and I would become partners in a new heating company, which I would set up and run in London, England. The thought of moving the family again made me very anxious, but on checking with them they seemed to think it would be fun to return to the UK, so I agreed.

We packed and shipped the furniture again, we

arranged to have it shipped by sea, and we flew to London; this was in early 1959. There we found accommodations in a hotel on Edgeware Road, which was close to Marble Arch.

I started checking with architects and large general contractors to acquaint them with our business card and a brief description of the type of services we were proposing to offer.

In the head office of Sir Lindsay Parkinson, a very large civil engineering contractor, I made the acquaintance of the Chief Architect called Leslie Walden. We became friends immediately. We had lunch and arranged to meet next day. He advised me that the board had made the decision that they could not deal with a new company, but would reconsider once we had established a reputation. He then asked me if I was looking for accommodations. When I answered yes, he told me that his next door neighbor, a mechanical engineer with Shell Oil Co. had been ordered to Amsterdam and the house was available for rent. We all drove down to inspect the place and liked it very much. Good schools were close by and Featherbed Lane was a well-kept neighborhood. Leslie Walden turned out to be quite a character. He was, among many other things, a gourmet cook, and I enjoyed many wonderful meals and fabulous wines with him. We must have visited every riverside restaurant within forty miles of home. The ladies decided to do their own thing while we enjoyed our outings. Sadly, Leslie died while on holiday in Majorca with his family.

I eventually met my younger brother, Ronald. So many years had passed that I had great difficulty in recognizing him.

Ronald introduced me to a company that built residential-type boilers, both gas and coal fired, and who was looking for experts to install them, together with small-bore heating in both residential and smaller commercial buildings. They were very pleased to listen to us, and eventually we signed an installation contract.

On returning home one day, I found Wendy in tears and Margaret consoling her. Apparently this rather forbidding-looking head mistress had taken exception to Wendy's mode of dress and demanded in a harsh voice that Wendy refrain from wearing nylon stockings and wearing bright and gaudy dresses. Margaret dealt with it and I never asked how!

Margaret and I looked out the window one day only to see Wendy climbing onto the back of a motorcycle. The young fellow driving it was Mike McDermott — more on Mike later.

Don came to stay with us for a couple of days and brought Stephanie, his daughter, with him as she had to get back to school in St. Andrews in Scotland. As I was driving them to Kings Cross, the main railway station from London direct to Edinburgh and on to St. Andrews, I heard poor Stephanie crying her heart out and being sick all over the back of the car. My first reaction was a cold rage at Don for condemning this delightful little girl to a school she hated and to be left to go there on her own in a strange country. I called him for every bad name I could think of and threatened him with violence; meantime we drove all through London with Stephanie's clothes hanging out the car window to dry.

In the meantime I had joined a flying club in Biggin Hill, a famous airfield used in WWII. We flew a trainer plane called a Miles Maggie. It had a double open cockpit and was a low wing monoplane. The first time I went up in the aircraft with the pilot instructor I strapped on the leather helmet with attached mike, tightened my seat harness, and we took off. What a sensation! At the end of the runway the cliff dropped six hundred feet and the updraft threw us into the air; next the pilot told me to take over. Unfortunately he had omitted to warn me that all the controls were delicate and required a very light touch. I grabbed the joystick and all hell broke loose. I put the light plane into a screaming dive and with my ability to act like lightening, I proceeded to yank the joystick up and down to try to correct my error, all during which the instructor and I were battling each other for possession of the joystick and he was screaming oaths in my helmet mike telling me to let it go. He and I had a wordy session when we landed and I told him that he was a damned fool for not warning me of the necessity of a very light touch on the controls. After that I decided that Terra Firma was the way for me to go and quit amateur flying.

We were awarded a heating project in Kent. Once I organized the installation I drove off to check progress on other projects. Three days later I had a call from the owners with a complaint that my mechanics had finished the job and left the premises, but a floorboard in the upper floor bedroom had been left loose. I immediately instructed my superintendent to proceed at once to rectify the problem. The house was a beautiful Tudor-style mini-mansion in manicured grounds and the owners were both professors at a local university. At around eight-thirty that night, I got a call from the very irate owners to tell me that water was pouring downstairs at a rapid rate and that one ceiling was already filled with water and about to burst. I asked them to shut the main valve to the system off, but being academics they were unaware of the way the system worked. I assured them that I would leave immediately and deal with the problem. On arrival at the house, I found the front door open and no one at home. I raced upstairs as water poured down and took one look at the bedroom floor and saw at once that my superintendent had nailed the floorboards through the floor and through the center of the water pipe underneath. With the heating on, it had magnified the size of the nail hole, and hence the flood. After clearing away as much debris as I could, I went looking for the owners and found them in the lounge of a local pub "drowning their sorrows" as they put it.

After apologizing and promising to rectify the damage, I arrived home about 1 a.m., cold, wet, and with a cold rage at the sheer stupidity of my superintendent, whom I promptly fired next morning. I felt dreadful, as their home was a monument of beauty and good taste and some of the furniture and drapes that were damaged were irreplaceable.

Don arrived at my office to check progress and discuss the future and asked, "Where is the toilet?" I took him to the window and showed him the outside privy in the back garden, which was three floors down. He picked up the morning paper and departed. Some time passed before I heard a tremendous uproar in the garden — it appeared that Don's behind had frozen to the toilet seat and when he finally managed to free himself he tried to wipe himself off with "Izal" — which was waxed square sheets of toilet paper — and in the process, smeared his behind. This type of toilet paper was quite popular in the U.K. at this time. I, of course, found this hilarious. We walked to the pub across the road, where Don desperately tried to get next to the tiny gas fire but the locals would not give way, so he ordered a glass of red wine and spilled half of it on the floor as his hands were shaking with the cold. We ordered lunch and of all things, he had ordered consomme from the cold menu. Was he miserable! I, of course, was close to being hysterical, which did not help.

Wendy and Mike's relationship at this time seemed to have cooled off, but both Margaret and I liked him and he kept in touch.

After two years in London, I realized that we were really ten years ahead of our time with this type of work. Some of the comments were, "But I must have the windows open to get fresh air." Battling that type of thinking was very disheartening. I called Don and told him that I thought that we were just spinning wheels and not making major progress. My feeling being that we should cut our losses and close the business — he agreed. I went ahead and flew back to Montreal.

Margaret followed by boat, and was I surprised when I met them at the dockyard in Montreal, as Mike was with them. It seems after talking to his boss that they had an opening for him in a company they owned in Montreal, and he had been intrigued by all the stories we had told him and decided to seize the opportunity. His first venture was a disaster, but on changing companies he did so well with his new company over the years that he became Vice President. He kept in touch and we had many happy times together. We had our usual miserable Montreal spring weather with a thaw and bitter cold spell and while driving downtown I braked and slid into a taxi with consequent front-end damage. Mike immediately offered me the use of his Mini Cooper car, and I accepted. On arriving home I charged the snow bank at our garage entrance, expecting as usual to smash my way through as I always did with the big heavy Ford station wagon. Alas, I ended up perched on the top of the snow bank six feet in the air with all four wheels spinning uselessly. My landlord and his two sons came out of the house laughing their heads off and further humiliated me by taking pictures before bodily lifting the car, with me inside it, off the snow bank.

I moved into the office and found to my dismay that Don, in his so-called wisdom, had altered the company name slightly and removed most of the working capital. This left the company close to bankruptcy. I worked long, hard hours and eventually got the company into reasonable shape. Unfortunately it had affected my family life. I approached Don and requested a thirty-six dollar a week raise. After a very acrimonious session and lots of drinking, he was adamant in refusing my request, and when I gave him two-week's notice, he said, "I guess I made a mistake."

My next job was the Queen Elizabeth Hotel in downtown Montreal, where I was offered the job of Assistant Superintendent. That was my lucky day! I met two mechanical engineers with whom I started to discuss aspects of the job. I had checked the drawings and the theory behind the design of some machinery and thought of a better way to use it. They agreed and we became very good friends, and from them I learned a great deal. They called me to their office one day and suggested that I study engineering at McGill University. I was stunned at first, but they insisted that I had the ability to better myself there. I took their advice and enjoyed a great learning experience.

The Queen Elizabeth project was quite large and very interesting mechanically, because of its location above the main CNR Railway Station in the center of Montreal and the fact that we had to connect a great many of the adjacent buildings to the new lines we ran from the big power station downtown. This was my first experience of lifting major air-conditioning and heating equipment on to the roof by helicopter. Major mechanical stations had to be built on every tenth floor to make sure that excess pressure was not generated in the guest rooms, as the building became higher and higher. One unfortunate incident occurred as we topped out the twenty-fourth floor. A deranged doctor climbed the open iron stairs and threw himself down onto the naked steel concrete reinforcing bars thirteen floors below. The mess was incredible, as was the feeling of horror generated by the loss of life.

Another major incident happened on the twelfth floor as they were pouring concrete. The mechanic driving a buggy full of cement drove too fast close to the edge of the building and hit the retaining wall, which caused the bucket to tilt and throw the whole load of wet cement onto Sherbrook Street, where both people and cars for a large area were covered with wet concrete.

I was having a beer in a bar on Sherbrook Street on my way home one evening when I struck up a conversation with a fellow from Paris, France. In the course of conversation, I learned that he taught a form of judo at a club on Atwater Street. I asked about joining and he said, "welcome." After getting the hang of the basics I seemed to be a natural and enjoyed the competitive spirit that prevailed. At one interclub competition I noticed something different about the matches a female was participating in. After carefully watching, I spotted her employing a dirty trick. I warned her twice quietly not to do so, but on being ignored, I requested a bout with her from the Master. He agreed and when she tried the trick on me, I blocked her and then let her taste her own medicine!

She staggered off the mat and left, never to return. The Master never chastised me, but his look was enough to let me know that he knew what had been going on and agreed with my action.

The hotel project was completed and I was looking around for another project, something rather large for preference. I liked large projects, as they presented more challenge and interest.

I had by this time established a very good reputation in Montreal. I was offered a job as manager of a new mechanical division of an air conditioning company. I had by this time all the Master licenses for plumbing, steamfitting and air-conditioning, plus I had recently qualified as a Canadian Quantity Surveyor, which all helped to establishing the new business.

My first project was a bid on a Kraft Paper Mill in Northern Quebec, which we were awarded. It being a multi-million dollar job we were very pleased. My troubles started with a willing but poorly knowledgeable superintendent. To get to see him once a week was imperative. Unfortunately, it was mid-winter when we started. I had to fly from Montreal to Monjolie, hire a car, and then drive 150 miles over iced-up mountain roads. You had to maintain a speed of 55 miles per hour on the icy roads or you could not get up the next hill. If you slid off the road for any reason, no one could stop to help without joining you in your predicament. What the truckers did on seeing your predicament, on their arrival at their destination after checking the location of the accident, was to alert the bulldozer driver of your problem; he then would, when the weather allowed, go out and pull you back onto the road. If your car was too badly damaged it was left there until spring. Another problem was the big trailer trucks hauling logs for the mill; they created a severe vacuum on passing them and forced you to adjust the steering and speed to offset the suction effect that they created. This proved mentally and physically exhausting.

Once at the site I had to work all through the night walking the project, catching errors and making drawings to illustrate how I wanted the job done. As there was no accommodation on site for visitors I would have breakfast with my superintendent, explain what was required, and then drive back to Monjolie and fly back to Montreal. I found it very exhausting.

The next project was the renovation of part of the Belmont Hotel in Bermuda — which I enjoyed very much. Unfortunately the family could not come with me, as the children's schooling would have been disturbed. We decided to go through the Caribbean Islands looking for projects. On arriving in Barbados we contacted the local engineer and learned that a major project was up for bid. We were successful and after serious discussion and just before signing the contract we were asked how much we had allowed for him — shocked, we cancelled everything and headed home.

On returning to Montreal from Bermuda we were engaged in a number of projects, nearly all of which were financially successful. On requesting a modest raise, I was harangued by the boss with the fact that if he gave me a raise he would have to give it to the others, so the answer was "no" — naturally I quit!

I called an acquaintance I had made in Bermuda. He said he was looking for a manager for the installation of the mechanical apparatus for three new hotels in Nassau, in the Bahamas.

I flew to the company headquarters in Norfolk and after being thoroughly grilled on my capabilities, then wined and dined royally, I picked up the drawings and flew to Nassau.

The company had rented a very nice house on the beach for executives. I set about getting office space organized, checked the quality and quantity of labor available locally, and advised the head office that I would need a fair number of American mechanics. As we were installing several new type of sewage plants and water treatment plants, I requested that the office purchase a portable laboratory complete with a powerful microscope and ship it ASAP. As I was very familiar with checking the bacteria level in the sewage plants it would prove invaluable.

The next chore was preparing templates for the repetitive work and finding bodies to carry out the work. With all the equipment and auxiliary parts on the dock, the political situation changed dramatically. The local PLP party was elected with a clear majority. I was advised that all work permits would be withdrawn immediately. Sure enough, next day two armed policemen arrived at my office with instructions for me to be gone next day. I said, "No," they said, "We will be here to escort you onto the plane," and they did.

I arrived in Miami, checked into a hotel and after communicating with the head office in Norfolk, was told to rent a car and enjoy myself, but to call in every day. I toured all over Florida and enjoyed Sarasota very much.

I called a local contractor in Nassau that I had become friendly with and worked out a deal over the phone with him to purchase the contracts from us, provided that I give him help with the layout work that I had already completed. The company was delighted, as we were paid back invoice prices and losses were minimal.

I was then directed to fly to Bermuda and go to work there. The Bermuda manager was part Cherokee Indian and had a violent temper and we were clashing frequently. Some of the work we did was interesting and the social life was wonderful. By this time Margaret and the girls had joined me. Our original accommodation was terrible and through a stroke of luck a lady Margaret knew spoke for us, and we were delighted to get this cottage right on the shores of Hungry Bay. The beaches were superb, as was the view of the ocean and three miles of reefs from our porch.

A major disturbance broke out and the Governor, together with his dog and his aide, were shot and killed at Government House from ambush. Segregation, which was still in effect at this time, had created a very bad atmosphere.

Riots broke out and the "back of town" was set on fire!

Our manager went to the hospital with a heart attack. I came into the office one day and found the secretary packing up the typewriter and associated paperwork. I asked what she was doing and was told that the manager had ordered her to take everything to his room at the hospital and they would do the office work from there. I said, "No way, the damned fool will have another attack." The upshot being that he discharged himself from the hospital, returned to the office, and gave me immediate notice to quit with two weeks' salary.

I drove into town and something told me to check in with B.A.C., a local air-conditioning company. I put a proposition to them and after two days they accepted it. This turned out to be one of my better moves.

I started my department with a clean sheet and no one with any knowledge of my business. I had built up a reputation for good work and a bad temper where ignorance was concerned. I even taught night school in order to better the quality of the local workmen. I had no trouble getting the best mechanics available. As word travelled around, I was flooded with requests from the employees at my previous company for a chance to work with me again. I was ecstatic.

We rapidly gained a good reputation, and we were flooded with work. The influx of the Re-Insurance Companies started due to a tax loophole in the USA, and large office blocks were being built. Computers in those days required special floor spaces and had to have very rigidly controlled temperature and humidity conditions. At last I was in my element with decent-sized jobs and a very good financial era starting. Money was a secondary object.

Due to the influx of so much construction, housing also boomed. With the demand for labor and the difficulty of getting work permits, I started our own night school — this paid off very well.

Once it became known abroad that there were no income taxes, no capital gains tax, etc., we became besieged with requests for work.

Out of the blue, Mr. Ludwig, of Greek shipping fame, wanted to build a new hotel. Once all fees and permits were dealt with, Mr. Ludwig convened a meeting with all concerned. His original idea was to build the Southampton Princess hotel with three hundred and fifty rooms, and a further three hundred rooms to be built in two years' time.

Mr. Ludwig said, "You gentlemen are going to take two years to build 350 rooms, but if you can build the whole six hundred and fifty in two years, I can recover my costs that much quicker." We agreed with a completely new contract and built-in penalty and bonus clause.

We were working with an American contractor, which was vital as the project was too large to be handled by us alone. The difficulty started with the American company wanting to install their own manager and I was adamantly against this. I was both familiar with large jobs and with contract law, plus I knew that local law stated that all joint venture projects must have a local director. I won out but at considerable cost, as bickering started on day one, and only ceased when the project was completed.

I was given a check for ten thousand dollars and all pleading for more was ignored. I developed a very cordial relationship with the local contractor's bookkeeper and managed to get my financial monthly draws in time to meet our commitments.

On checking the pumps recently shipped to the site, I was immediately aware that we had a problem. My calculations showed them to be inadequate to pump liquid to the height the site situation required. When I brought this up to our co-partner's attention, I was treated with blank stares and the point was ignored. Next meeting was the same. Having spent all my spare time checking all available information, I blew up and in no uncertain terms demanded that this information be entered into the minutes of the next meeting. The upshot being the demand from the overseas owner for a major meeting on the subject. I was told in no uncertain terms that they would demand my removal. I knew that the owner was an exceptionally smart engineer and if I could persuade him to check my figures I would be vindicated and the error would be corrected. The costs involved in re-shipping the equipment back out of the country were distorting the minds of the people I was dealing with. Mr. Kent, the owner, and I never got along as he had been listening to his own prejudiced people. Next day all hell broke loose, orders were flying all over the place, and the chief engineer was flown in from Miami. All this without a word to me, but I did not give a damn as I was certain that I was correct in my calculations.

Johnny the engineer arrived from Miami, and on checking my work called a meeting and told all and sundry that I was correct in all details and that there was one drawing that his office had not received; this caused the error. Next he turned to me and congratulated me for having gone into so many minor details and for having even checked the specific gravity of the water at the temperature at which we would be pumping it.

I realized that I had made some bitter enemies, but I was so disturbed that I would not back down. Strangely enough, Bob Kent, with his lady friend, had dinner with Margaret and me whenever we met in Florida in the future.

Our landlady died and her son offered to sell us the house. As we discussed the price, I asked him if he would accept my half acre as part payment, he agreed, and we settled that at forty thousand dollars. I was happy at the profit and when he quoted a total for the house of eighty thousand dollars I wrote him a check immediately and called our lawyer to finalize the details.

We were ecstatic, but I wondered if I had bitten off more than I could handle, but cash flow never wavered and we carried on.

The owner of a very attractive restaurant called Henry the Eighth, which proved very popular with us, had a brain-wave and decided to stage a Saturday night special event at which a properly attired fourteenth century king and queen would preside. All food and wine would be served as is. This meant whole fish, fowl, and haunches of meat were served on platters in the center of the table with each participant given only a large knife with which to carve chunks out of the carcasses, etc. Serving wenches, suitably dressed, kept the wine goblets replenished. Partway through the ceremony several of us were ceremoniously knighted by the reigning king and a good time was had by all. Next morning was a different story, as most of us were wandering around holding our heads and bemoaning our fate. Needless to say, this type of entertainment was very popular with us, but the landlord of the establishment regretted his decision and ceased after the third time around.

In 1967, Wendy and Paul decided to marry. The U.S. authorities seemed to take forever checking all our historic details. Then Carol and David decided to marry. Late that year both girls were married within three weeks of one another. It proved to be a nerve-wracking time and adjusting to the empty house took a while.

On completion of the project, an opening-night party was held in the main ballroom of the Southampton Hotel. This was a magnificent event with a hundred waiters walking around the perimeter, each with a flaming baked Alaska dessert on his shoulder.

When it came time to collect our bonus, all hell broke loose — we were accused of all kinds of nonsense and I calmly asked Mr. Ludwig's lawyers to read the contract that he had signed. They paid up!

I had put up with far too much nonsense from all and sundry, so when the managing director of BAC placed one of his cronies in charge of the company, I asked him to fire the guy, as I knew that he was incapable of doing the job properly. I said, "Give me the job." He refused and said maybe we should just form a new company for your division. I said, "No way, I am going to form my own company, and if you do not step on my toes I will not step on yours!"

I had of course, obtained Bermuda Status prior to this time and had no difficulty registering the company, which I called Atlantic Engineering Ltd. This was in 1973.

We went from success to success and began to prosper. One of my better mechanics was working on a problem one day when I asked him if he needed help. He refused, saying, "I have the answer, thanks to you." He then said, "You have turned around all the companies you have worked for, so I know that yours will be successful." Those words have stuck with me all these years!

A friend of mine, Durham Stevens, had offered me a half acre near the water, complete with an orchard full of local bananas and grapefruit for twenty five thousand dollars — I jumped at it!

As we prospered we brought Margaret's mother over for a visit. Poor dear, she was overwhelmed at the way we lived and while she enjoyed every minute with us, she refused to come again. We helped Margaret's brother Bill's son go to college and sit for his C.A.'s exam. We also brought over the rest of Margaret's family for annual holidays, which we all enjoyed a great deal.

As the house on Hungry Bay was so attractive we were reluctant to start building a new one on the half acre that Durham had sold us. We had a great view of the ocean where we were and had a great view of the offshore reefs with an almost constant southwest breeze. We were located seventy feet above sea level and close to two hundred yards back from the seashore — a perfect location. As we made money, we put into action our ideas of how the house would develop. First we expanded sideways and installed a decent laundry area with a workshop underneath for me. Next we pulled in a bulldozer to level the backyard and install a swimming pool. We installed fancy lights and above water level two jets which when controlled gave us a delightful background burble. As we were excavating the pool, I realized that we had space for a decent sized pump room and space for a sauna, which we promptly ordered and installed. As time went by, Margaret suggested that we build a patio out from the garage. We did and realized that we had created room for an apartment. When that was completed we were delighted. We then built a shelter for the car over the cesspit. As we had good acreage we had the place landscaped, which Margaret happily took charge of. Wendy and Paul meantime had been moved by his division to a base in Albuquerque, New Mexico, and had invited us to visit them. We flew down in several different aircraft, the last one piloted by a guy in high cowboy boots and a ten-gallon hat. The airline was referred to as "last chance airlines." We met some very interesting people and enjoyed a trip into Mexico at El Paso. We were introduced to a father and son team that ran a glider school. The father had been a fighter pilot on an aircraft carrier during WWII, so we swapped stories. We were invited to go flying in the glider and enjoyed the very different sensation. As Margaret took off for her turn in the glider the father approached me with an offer to fly me in the twelve-cylinder engine tow plane. No one had told me that he was an expert exhibitionist and a stunt pilot to boot. I had told him some of my experiences flying with bush pilots in Northern Canada. We took off and he promptly turned the plane upside down and flew around like that for a few minutes. This was again an open cockpit type aircraft and my gut was giving me hell — next thing I knew we were flying upside down over the ridge of the roof of the aircraft hangar and only six feet above it. What an experience that was. While in Mexico we were astonished at the amount of poverty visible. Paul called over an urchin and told him, "Here is five dollars, will you make sure that no one strips our car before we return?" He agreed and in two minutes a gang of youths surrounded our car. We returned later to find it intact in every detail. Paul said that it was worth another five bucks.

The Southampton Princess Hotel was designed with a high-pressure fresh water flash evaporating type plant and was supplied by brackish water pumped from underground wells, one hundred and fifty feet down the hill. The water was very brackish and we discovered that when pumping, large quantities of sand were being pumped along with the water. I called the engineer with a description of the problem and suggested a solution. He agreed and I submitted plans, which he endorsed. We built a large concrete box with numerous concrete baffles to separate the sand from the water. We also had a problem with excessive amounts of hydrogen sulfide, which is missible with oxygen, so we lifted the concrete roof and supported it with columns leaving large openings well above water level and got rid of the hydrogen sulfide to the atmosphere. This would have destroyed all metal it came in contact with if we had not acted. Some sand escaped, and we experienced severe erosion of the internal baffle plates in the flash evaporator section of the water treatment plant. The only answer was to order them made of titanium metal — that worked.

Late one night I had a call from the hotel engineer to say that the sewage plant was in trouble and could I come now. I drove down to the plant and the engineer gave me a pair of rubber boots, which were required as the whole area was covered in a brown filthy stinking sludge which was still pouring over the lip of the retaining channel of the plant. The operator had fled in panic. As I walked into the mess to start to ascertain what the problem was, I felt the grunge leaking into my boot; when I turned around the engineer was convulsed with laughter as he was famous for practical joking. I knew what he had done. My boot had a large slit at the back of it and was leaking copious amounts of stinking sludge.

After a period of checking and searching I noticed that there was a very large quantity of small feathers and lots of oil in the mix. This made me think kitchen. On arriving in the kitchen we summoned all the staff out of bed and questioned them at length. Suddenly the head chef said that he had fired a Portuguese dishwasher and noticed him and a fired waiter hanging around after dinner. It appeared that together they had burst a feather pillow and stuffed it down the kitchen drain together with a forty-gallon drum of cooking oil. It took us nearly two days with a full crew to eradicate the oil and clean up the mess. When I presented the bill they added a bonus, as we had saved the hotel from having to close.

My secretary called me to take a phone call and I had a real shock when Don Storey, of all people, asked me to be his best man when he next came to Bermuda. I took the opportunity to remind him that as I had told him frequently, "I was the best man." We had a good laugh at that. When we met he told me he was opening an office in Bermuda and would Margaret like to be his secretary. I said, "Ask her." He hired her immediately and then set about getting office space, etc.

As we could take the time, Margaret and I traveled to different places. The first was to Fairbanks in Alaska; I wanted to check out the method used to install the oil pipeline from the Yukon to the oil terminal at Anchorage. I was fascinated to note that the pipeline supports were cooled by air-conditioning units powered by the sun. This was carried out to avoid heat by induction, which would cause the supports to sink into the permafrost and damage the pipe. We then carried on to Denali Park and rented a helicopter to take us over the area and to take us as far up the glacier as possible. What an awe-inspiring sight. We were very fortunate to see the peak of the Denali Mountain clearly for about ten minutes. The peak is twenty-four thousand feet high. We then went on to pick up the Holland America cruise ship from Anchorage to Vancouver. We met my brother Charles and his wife in Victoria on Vancouver Island, but had great difficulty in communicating with one another. He had lived a very quiet suburban-type existence while I had traveled the world and seen many aspects of life in many different countries. His primary topic of conversation was about lawn bowling.

I was desperate to find a manager, as I was working seven days a week and often with only four hours of sleep. I flew to London and advertised for help. I hired what I thought was a perfect guy in London, he had been a guardsman and was well educated. I wined and dined he and his family and formed a good impression, then flew him to Bermuda, where I dropped him off at a local landlady's house for the night. On checking him out after dinner he was nowhere to be seen. The landlady said the last time she saw him, he was walking down the road with his suitcase in hand. I looked everywhere and then had an inspiration — what if that swine was at the airport? And on the way home I told Margaret what I thought, and she said, "You're crazy, he would never do a thing like that." I stormed off to the airport and there he was waiting for the next flight back to the UK. All I could see in my fury was blood red. I savagely butted him in the face with my head then kneed him where it hurt most, and when I asked him what the hell he was playing at? His reply left me speechless. He said, "I am not living with Spics, etc." God, what a mistake I had made!

I came home one day to find Mike McDermott happily sipping wine on the porch with Margaret. What a pleasant surprise! We discovered that he was vice-president of his company and would be in Bermuda quite often on business. We were very happy to see him again.

I had a call at two a.m. one morning from the engineer at the Southampton Hotel to tell me he had guests complaining that they had lumps of tar in their bathwater. I thought he was drunk and told him to sleep it off. The phone rang shortly after and I heard the General Manager's voice before I went to hang up. He sounded desperate. He said, "We have lumps of tar in all the bathtubs, and we will have to evacuate the hotel." I told him, "Do nothing until I arrive." I awakened Margaret and asked her to call out all my men and tell them we had a major emergency. We were, of course, in the middle of a tropical storm with heavy rain and wind. When I arrived at the site and checked the bathrooms I was finally convinced it was not a hoax. After talking quickly to the manager, I went outside and walked all over the grounds seeking an answer. On climbing up to the major dining room roof I found it flooded with all kinds of debris and the outlet choked solid. As I worked in the deluge to clear the outlet I became aware that I was covered in a filthy black sticky substance. I ran down to the boiler room and stripped down, when I went to hang my clothes up near the boiler to dry I found them covered in black tar. I have to divert a moment to explain that all roofs in Bermuda are painted white and act as a fresh water catch, there being very little fresh water available on the island. On going back outside with a large flashlight, I discovered five fifty-gallon empty paint drums. It appeared that the senior company engineer in New York had been able to buy them cheaply and not being aware that he was introducing toxic poison to the hotel drinking water instructed a local painting contractor to paint the roof with tar.

We had a major problem as the main roof was drained by a twelve-inch diameter cast iron pipe with all auxiliary roofs joined into it on the way down. Careful checking led us to the solution. We had to smash a large hole in the wine storage room, of all places, then cut into the main down pipe and divert the water to drain outside the building — this with tropical conditions at their worst. When I inspected the one-million gallon fresh water storage tank it was a disaster. The tank had three divisions with the walls stopping two feet below the roof. I called my friend Arthur Whalley, who was a certified diver and asked for help. On his arrival I briefed him and called for all the water truckers on the island for help. As each truck arrived we started them pumping out the contaminated water from the tank sections. Arthur meantime was skimming the tar off the water surface and handing it out to the laborers.

We were fortunate to find one section of the tank with very little tar floating on the water surface and decided that this section was recoverable.

Once the tank was cleaned we then had to have the roof completely cleared of tar and recoated properly before we could reconnect the main piping. The manager had his staff serving our crew food and drink and helped by changing everyone's wet and filthy clothes, and handing out clean boiler suits.

The manager was so pleased that he gave Margaret and I the full use of the honeymoon suite with flowers and champagne for the weekend. The costs of the whole proceeding were tremendous but the hotel management did not hesitate to write a check in full.

Margaret meantime went off and organized financial conferences in Vienna, Geneva, and New York for Don Storey, who had by this time bought and published a monthly booklet called *The Bank Credit Analyst,* which became in great demand by the international financial community.

Margaret and I were able to take some trips abroad. We went to Alaska, a cruise on the River Rhine, and a two-week tour of Switzerland, among others. Don Hunt, a very good friend, came up with a business proposal that looked very interesting on the Island of Providenciales in the Turks and Caicos chain. A number of us were invited to join in the venture. I took ten percent. Don charted a private jet for the journey and gave us a glowing report on progress. He had also arranged a Canadian Government loan to build a forty-thousand square foot warehouse. On the next trip we all went with him by private jet and had a great deal of fun. When climbing into our beds we had to pour a whole bottle of Six-Twelve bug-repellant over the mosquito netting as the no-see-um bugs were rampant — as were the mosquitoes. On piling into the rental car the next day to view the site we were quite shocked to see the warehouse being started, but there was no sign of a signed contract to start the project. We were assured that it would be signed shortly and told not to worry. On checking around and considering the time and money already spent I knew that something was seriously out of hand. Further reflection strengthened my thinking, and I made the decision to abandon my share of the project. Lorenzo, my friend, agreed and we talked the pilot of the private jet into giving us a lift back to his home base in Buffalo in the USA, from which we returned to Bermuda. Subsequently we learned that the project went belly up at great expense.

Don Storey bought a yacht which he called Blackhawk, a Bermuda forty-foot ketch, which was located in Fire Island, NY. I went through the vessel thoroughly and found a flaw in the forestay. On reporting the problem to Don, I suggested that he install roller furling to the new forestay, and he agreed. When ready to sail, I told Don to call the Customs for clearance to Bermuda. When he refused I washed my hands of the whole thing and took a flight home to Bermuda. While I was a guest many times on his yacht, in the harbor, I would never sail with him.

He proved my judgment correct when in a gale somewhere off Newport he jibed the boat and dismasted her. He made matters worse and extremely dangerous, as with all the masts and wire rigging over the side and banging on the hull, he started the engine and on putting it in gear wrapped wire cables around the shaft and propeller, thus disabling the yacht completely. I understand that one of the crew volunteered to go overboard and cut the wreckage loose and in doing so was badly injured in the extremely rough seas.

I had purchased a Tartan twenty-seven foot yacht and enjoyed sailing around the island and spending the weekend aboard plus racing it offshore. I wanted to sail it to Annapolis and spent considerable time preparing it for the ocean crossing. One fellow came with me to assist. Two days out we were hit with a freak storm and it continued interminably. As my so-called assistant was violently seasick, I left him in the cabin and strapped myself into the cockpit. It took eight and a half days to reach the Chesapeake lightship. As I was totally exhausted, I called Earl up from below and told him to stay in sight of the lightship. It was foggy and raining with poor visibility, but I needed two hours sleep to be in condition to navigate the north entrance to the City of Refuge, at the mouth of the Chesapeake Bay. On awakening exactly two hours later, I could not identify a thing — my language was unprintable. We were jumping and tossing about in gale force winds when suddenly I spotted the tip of one of the Chesapeake bridge towers, but it was in the wrong place. When I looked at the chart I was dismayed; the damned fool had not only lost sight of the lightship but gotten us into a narrow sand channel with no outlet. I checked all around and noticed on the chart that there was a sandbar with a shallow center close by. On checking the height of the tide at that time I figured that with the centerboard up and the engine full out we might make it back to the deep water channel. I took the tiller and gunned her, we felt the bump as we hit the crest, but we were through. We pulled into a dock and I phoned the Customs office in Norfolk for clearance and on returning to the boat found my assistant all packed and standing on the dock in the rain and saying not another step would he take on this boat. I had to forcibly restrain him until the customs officer had come aboard and issued our clearance to land together with our cruising permit. I called on the marina manager to ask where the restaurant was and was told that it had been closed but that they had an arrangement with a restaurant five miles away. The upshot being that he would drive me there and the lady proprietor of the eatery would drive me back to the yacht. On arrival I created quite a stir as I ordered a large porterhouse steak with all the trimmings and two double scotch whiskeys in one glass. I discovered later that I had lost sixteen pounds on the trip.

As I left port alone on my way up the Chesapeake Bay to Annapolis, I noticed a tug boat pulling a barge up channel so decided to follow him as I was still suffering deep fatigue from the ocean trip and this would save me navigating my way up-channel. After a half hour passed, I noticed that I had massacred a pile of insects with my wet towel. The whole cockpit was covered with them and I could not breathe without swallowing mouthfuls of them. When I looked up I saw all the crew of the tugboat laughing their heads off at my predicament. I immediately realized that I had been foolish enough to get behind a tug with a garbage disposal unit returning from dumping their load of sewage in the open ocean. I pulled clear and gunned the engine — on passing the tug I was subjected to some ribald good-humored joking.

Hugh, my friend, had told me to watch for a special buoy with a green flashing light as I approached the Annapolis channel entrance, which would keep me clear of a shoal as I turned for the entrance to the West River. Suddenly I see green lights flashing all over the starboard side. On getting over my shock I realized a bunch of fire flies were passing over my starboard navigation light, which is green. I cleared the bad shoal and made my way upriver to Hugh Wallis's pier in Gainsville, but being so dreadfully fatigued I made a wrong turn and ended in a cove I did not recognize, so I let go the anchor and shut down the engine, and as I was pulling up the anchor light, Hugh in his yacht with Margaret and others aboard appeared and ribbed the hell out of me for getting lost on his doorstep, so to speak. I up-anchored and followed him around the corner and gratefully moored the yacht at his wharf. Margaret had joined me in Annapolis, and we cruised all over the Chesapeake Bay and enjoyed the local seafood immensely. The myriad bays and inlets were a joy to cruise in as was the hospitality of our many friends in the area.

Margaret flew home, and a friend of mine had flown out to help me to sail the yacht home. We made the return journey in four and a half days. One day out from Bermuda had presented us with a magnificent view of the tall ships in full sail coming out of the early morning mist led by the white-sailed square-rigged Russian tall ship called the *Krushenstern*. The copy of the log of that trip makes for some hilarious reading.

I was frequently asked to navigate in the large off-shore yacht races from Newport to Bermuda and enjoyed doing so. The people from Woods Hole used to come to the pre-race conferences and provided us with pictures of the latest movements of the Gulf Stream. This was invaluable, as a wrong move in one of the breakaway meanders would slow the boat down enough to destroy any hope of winning the race. We had some very exciting moments, but all in all we had a great deal of fun. I also learned much more about the antics of the Gulf Stream and the Labrador Current that runs under it on parts of the American East Coast.

One incident stays permanently etched in my mind. I was asked by a good friend to navigate for him in the annual amateur yacht race from Newport to Bermuda. We left Bermuda in heavy weather and were on the starboard tack for two and a half days before I got a look at the sun. I was shocked to find us seventy-five miles east of the rumb line. The Captain then took over and told me that I did not know what I was doing. I went below in a very confused state of mind, but when I heard him taking a bearing on the Cape Cod AM radio station, I realized that he had no knowledge of radio frequency distortion over the land. I searched every helmsman for anything metallic in their pockets; no luck. On getting a quick glimpse of the sun and a second sight it confirmed my first reckoning. I physically docked the Captain when he argued, sat him down in a corner of the cockpit, then told the helmsman to alter course one hundred and eight degrees and call me in eight hours, when he should see Nantucket Lightship. I went below but did not sleep. As directed he called me and when I asked him what light it was he said he did not know. I asked, "What the hell did I give him a stopwatch for?" On timing the light I was pleased to have called it correctly. In the meantime, the roller furling on the mainmast exploded and the sail went overboard. We finally got it aboard and jury-rigged the boom and mainsail and carried on to Newport. On climbing the steep ladder to the dock, I nearly walked off the dock and had to get off the dock on my hands and knees. The weather had been so bad all the way that we had lost the balance of our land legs. I insisted on having an official compass adjuster come aboard to check the compass. He did and ended up throwing his hat on the deck and jumping on it. He could not get the compass to work properly. We finally realized that the diamond setting into which the compass card pin was riding was chipped and jamming the compass card in one position. This could have gotten us all drowned. I told him not to worry as I planned to bring my own handheld compass for the return trip.

This yacht should never have been allowed to go to sea. Every joint leaked, and the top connection to the diesel fuel tank leaked diesel fuel into the bilge, which combined with all the other odors, made most of the crew seasick. Some joints in the woodwork rubbing together all the time created a cacophony of noise, making sleep impossible. I never sailed on her again.

We had purchased a condo in The Meadows in Sarasota, Florida, and enjoyed many breaks there. Around this time in 1999 I was starting to feel the tremendous strain of working 24/7 and made the decision to sell the company to my son-in-law David and his partner in 2001. I gave them a good deal, I thought, and looked forward to enjoying my retirement. I played golf regularly and sailed my new thirty-foot Tartan yacht in all the races, plus used it for pleasure cruises and parties.

Suddenly, I noticed Margaret complaining a great deal about small details and generally acting out of character. I told her she would have to change her attitude, but no change occurred. I took off for the U.K., bought a house in Edinburgh, and played every golf course within thirty miles of Edinburgh. I had a great time. I visited my friend in St. Briac, France, and checked out the reverse turbine in the river at St. Malo in France, toured the highlands of Scotland, etc. Margaret and the girls still came to the area to visit her family, and we met occasionally. I had a call one day from my brother Hamilton, asking me to meet him at Edinburgh airport. After standing around for half an hour or so I was beginning to think that I had been stood up, but on seeing an older looking bald-headed fellow holding a large rolled map-type package I walked over and asked his name — the answer was a blistering harangue at the time he had wasted waiting for me. This was our first meeting in twenty-five years, so recognition was to say the least shocking. Once we had settled down he said he was employed as a technician to check oil samples on ships carrying bulk oil cargoes all over the European coastline. Some of the ships' chief engineers had devised a way of using the oil cargo as bunker fuel and were pocketing the proceeds. He was equipped with a specially adapted computer that along with other auxiliary equipment was able to analyze the different oil samples. He would then provide the ship with samples and forward others to the head office for final analysis and appropriate action. He had been attacked on numerous occasions on different ships and was in the process of retiring. He handed me a copy of our family tree, and I found this remarkably interesting. A friend of his in the City of Inverness in Scotland, with the same family name as ours, on retiring went to the famous Tabernacle of the Mormons in Utah and made copies of all the information available, then spent a lot of years searching the micro films in the various Mormon-associated churches called the Church of the Latter Day Saints in the U.K. It appears that the Graydon family originated in France, and as they were of Huguenot per-suasion they were continually subjected to religious abuse and persecution and finally left for England, where they joined forces with Sir Oliver Cromwell and signed alle-giance to King Edgar. After allying with Robert the Bruce in his bid for the Scottish throne, which failed. The lands of Peter De Gradeen were confiscated and then ceded to the Monks of Durham Cathedral. The name over the centuries has altered numerous times but is now spelled Graydon. Various branches of the family are to be found in America, Canada, Australia, and New Zealand.

After about three years of carefree living in Edinburgh, I had a worried phone call from Wendy and Carol in Bermuda asking me to please come home quickly, as Margaret was showing definite signs of dementia. I immediately knew what I should have seen all along, that Margaret's behavior was an early indication of the onset of Alzheimer's disease. I berated myself for not catching on at the start, as her brother Jim died as a result of Parkinson's disease; also her sister Jean had died of Alzheimer's after a twelve-year bout with it. I had absolutely, no excuse as we had gone over every year to Scotland to see Jean and spend time with her. I was devastated. I sold off everything as fast as I could and returned to Bermuda to take care of Margaret.

Knowing that we could get much better quality care in the USA, I brought Margaret to our place in Sarasota and took her to see a specialist, where she was properly diagnosed with the disease. We did everything we could to make Margaret's life as happy and comfortable as we possibly could. I took Margaret to as many different points of interest to help keep her mind active. One day a Canadian golfing friend suggested that I take Margaret to Niagara Falls and stay at a Holiday Inn that he owned as his guests — we were ecstatic. As soon as we entered the room we realized that we were in the honeymoon suite and thought that this was great fun. As we lay down to rest after the hassle of flying, we had a telephone call from the front desk asking us how we spelled our name. I was upset as we had booked in properly and told them so. Finally the manager came to the door and explained that a newlywed couple with the same name as ours had booked the honeymoon suite and as we had checked in prior to their arrival the staff assumed that we were the honeymooners. We had a great laugh at this and ended up with a very nice room for the rest of our stay. Coping with Margaret's bizarre behavior finally became a nightmare, and the girls then advised me to find a good home for Margaret where they specialized in caring for people with her problem. I was devastated in doing this and suffered a great deal of guilt and remorse at doing this to someone I loved so dearly.

Margaret passed away in June 2007, was cremated, and we took her ashes back to Bermuda and cast them on the waters of Hungry Bay, her favorite swimming place. Our loss was devastating.

Carol, David, and their children and grandchildren all continue to live happily in Bermuda. Wendy and Paul live close by in Florida, as do my granddaughter Mandy, her husband, and children. Chris, my grandson, with his wife and daughters live in Maryland.

My dear sister Patricia moved to a town called Newmarket, which is located north of Toronto. Mike and Nancy McDermott were extremely kind and visited frequently, taking her out to lunch and generally cheered her up. Unfortunately she had a bad accident with her electric chair and eventually succumbed to her injuries. Wendy and I managed to visit her just prior to her passing on. I will forever remember Mike and Nancy's kindness to her.

Mike and Nancy live in Mississauga near Toronto in Canada. We continue to get together every year and enjoy a great relationship. We plan to spend two weeks with them in August this year and will visit Niagara-on-the-Lake together, where we intend to see a play by George Bernard Shaw. Mike and Nancy plan to visit us in November this year, as they do enjoy visiting us in Sarasota.

Roy and Pearl McLean, our longtime friends from Montreal, are always in our thoughts. We had many happy times together camping with them and their children in the mountains of northern New York State and with their visits to us in Bermuda.

Sadly, Pearl passed away recently. Roy is enjoying a break from the harsh Canadian winter here in Sarasota, and we have enjoyed his company. Unfortunately, he leaves shortly for home. We have enjoyed a visit from our friend Michael Spurling and his wife Vikki, who we knew very well in Bermuda. They now live in the USA. Our very good friends Brian and Fern Cullimore from Bermuda have a holiday home in Tampa, USA, but have now relocated permanently to the town of Victoria on Vancouver Island in Canada. We miss them very much, but do keep in touch. Our longtime friends from Montreal, Ken and Leone Biggs, relocated to Edmonton in Canada and they too keep in touch — we have promised to visit them in Jasper, Canada, next year.

Derek and Gerry Brashier, friends from Bermuda, have also moved to Sarasota and we have enjoyed their company on many occasions. Unfortunately Gerry has developed Alzheimer's disease and has had to be admitted to a medical facility. We continue to spend time with Derek socially.

We have arranged to meet Stephanie and Ray Storey-Vilaincou in Savannah, Georgia, in July this year. Stephanie is the eldest daughter of my late good friend Don Storey and lives in Texas with her husband Ray. They spend their summers in Prince Edward Island in Canada. They are very dear friends of ours, and we look forward to getting together with them once again.

I have, fortunately, met a very nice lady called Louise, who is a widow with two grown children. We enjoy life together very much and seem to have very similar tastes, which makes for a very comfortable relationship. We also have many mutual friends. Louise is a wonderful person to be with, and I must say that we have become very fond of each other. We each have our own homes which we enjoy.

My father was a very good mechanical engineer. During my early years the U.K. was in a very deep depression and work was difficult to obtain. My father went from one poor paying job to another and never made a decent living wage. One of his problems was the fact that he was a very mild-mannered man and hated to displease anyone. My mother was the exact opposite and seemed to make his life rather miserable at times.

My mother was a character, very bright mentally, very artistic, and somewhat devious with a terrible temper. That proved to be quite a combination. I vaguely recollect Mother making sweaters of very fine cashmere wool for a company in Paris, France. She used an easel with a large colored picture of the finished product, which was outlined in small squares in which she inserted colored pins to indicate the different designs of the pattern she was knitting. I found this fascinating. Mother also took in lodgers and rented rooms by the week, all to help increase their income. Mother was also a prodigious reader and was never without a book close by her. I can never, ever remember her fussing over any of us and myself in particular. I was always asking questions about how and why things worked, which seemed to aggravate her badly and made her prone to using violence. I became very adept at rolling with the punches so to speak, especially when she set about me with her favorite cast iron frying pan. In my later years, I came to realize that she must have been suffering badly from frustration with so many kids hanging around and getting in her way. She would have made a first class CEO, but definitely not in those days. Mother's work on tapestry-type needlework was a joy to behold, some of which we still have with us today. On Mother's side of the family we come from the Scottish Clan Lindsay, a sept of the Clan Crawford, which dates back to the tenth century. I understand that a Lindsay was elected poet laureate in the fourteenth century.

Apart from the campaign medals awarded to me for service in WWII, I was awarded the Arctic Star medal by the British Government in June 2013 for voyages made to assist Russia during WWII — a mere seventy years late, but very acceptable, and I am now in the process of being awarded a prestigious Russian Naval medal called the "Ushakov" medal, which is to be issued by the Russian government under direct authority of Premier Vladimir Putin for those of us who crewed ships on voyages with vital military supplies from the U.K. to Murmansk in Arctic Russia during WWII. The foregoing are more fully illustrated by the two episodes I have written and given speeches on — "The Voyage To Hell" and "The Role of the Convoy Rescue Ships During WWII" — to the American Master Mariners Association of Tampa, the American Merchant Seamen's Association of Bradenton, and also to the ladies of the British Empire Association in Sarasota.

On August the eleventh, 2014, Louise, Wendy, and I were invited to attend the Russian Embassy in Washington, DC, I, to be awarded the Russian Federation Naval "Ushakov" medal. It was a momentous moment for me and was carried out graciously by a member of the embassy staff. Refreshments were served following the ceremony. We were very upset that Wendy was unable to come with us and missed the ceremony.

Following the ceremony we spent ten days with Mike and Nancy in and around Mississauga. We traveled to Niagara-on-the-Lake and stayed at a wonderful hotel across from the large marina. Thanks to Mike and Nancy we saw a wonderful play, then carried on to see the falls from the ground and from the restaurant on the top of the revolving tower. The views were spectacular. The journey home was an anti-climax.